# BOMBER COMMAND

FAILED TO RETURN

Published in 2011 by Fighting High Ltd, 23 Hitchin Road,
Stotfold, Hitchin, Herts, SG5 4HP
www.fightinghigh.com

British Library Cataloguing-in-Publication data. A CIP record
for this title is available from the British Library.

ISBN 978 0 9562696 6 9

Designed by Michael Lindley www.truthstudio.co.uk.
Printed and bound by Toppan Printing Co. (UK) Ltd.

# BOMBER COMMAND
## FAILED TO RETURN

STEVE BOND, STEVE DARLOW, JULIAN EVAN-HART,
SEAN FEAST, ADAM PURCELL AND CHRISTOPHER YEOMAN

John X. Banfield MBE
207 Sqn
Ex-P.o.W.

Steve Darlow

FH

# CONTENTS

110

82

10

94

62

20

30

104

40

50

# FOREWORD

BY TONY IVESON, DFC, AE, CRAeS

IN THE HOUSE OF COMMONS ON 3 SEPTEMBER 1940, AT THE HEIGHT OF THE BATTLE OF BRITAIN, PRIME MINISTER WINSTON CHURCHILL SAID: 'THE NAVY CAN LOSE US THE WAR BUT ONLY THE AIR FORCE CAN WIN IT. THEREFORE OUR SUPREME EFFORT MUST BE TO GAIN OVERWHELMING MASTERY OF THE AIR. NOW, THE FIGHTERS ARE OUR SALVATION BUT THE BOMBERS ALONE PROVIDE THE MEANS TO VICTORY.' HE WENT ON TO DEMAND 'THE PULVERISATION OF THE ENTIRE INDUSTRY AND SCIENTIFIC STRUCTURE ON WHICH THE WAR EFFORT AND ECONOMIC LIFE OF THE ENEMY DEPEND'.

FOR THE FIRST TWO YEARS OF THE WAR, BOMBER COMMAND'S HEAVY LOSSES IN DAYLIGHT OPERATIONS CAUSED A SWITCH TO NIGHT ATTACKS, BUT FLYING AT NIGHT OVER A BLACKED-OUT GERMANY IN EUROPEAN WEATHER CONDITIONS WITH THE NAVIGATION AIDS THEN AVAILABLE MEANT TARGET LOCATION AND ACCURATE BOMBING WERE AT ALL TIMES VERY DIFFICULT AND MOSTLY IMPOSSIBLE. BUT BY 1942 FOUR-ENGINE BOMBERS WERE REACHING THE SQUADRONS IN INCREASING NUMBERS, AND ELECTRONIC NAVIGATIONAL EQUIPMENT BECAME AVAILABLE IN QUANTITY. THE FORMATION OF THE PATHFINDER FORCE OF EXPERIENCED AND HIGHLY TRAINED CREWS TO LOCATE AND MARK TARGETS LED TO A CONSIDERABLE IMPROVEMENT IN RESULTS.

BOMBER COMMAND WAS THE ONLY BRITISH FORCE THAT TOOK THE WAR INTO THE GERMAN HEARTLAND FOR FOUR LONG HARD-FOUGHT YEARS BETWEEN THE RETREAT FROM DUNKIRK IN 1940

AND THE INVASION OF FRANCE IN 1944. ITS PERSISTENCE IN MOUNTING CONTINUOUS ATTACKS ON GERMAN INDUSTRY, TRANSPORTATION, PORTS, OIL PRODUCTION, AND ENERGY SOURCES EVENTUALLY GAVE CHURCHILL HIS MASTERY OF THE AIR IN LATE 1944. BUT A DREADFUL PRICE HAD TO BE PAID AND THAT WAS THE LIVES OF OUR AIRCREW. OF THE 125,000 AIRCREW WHO SERVED IN BOMBER COMMAND, 60 PER CENT – OR THREE OUT OF FIVE – BECAME CASUALTIES, WITH MOST BEING KILLED. THEY WERE THE BEST OF OUR YOUNG MEN, IN PHYSICAL HEALTH, IN EDUCATION AND INTELLIGENCE IN LEARNING QUICKLY HOW TO OPERATE THEIR AIRCRAFT AND EQUIPMENT – AND IN THEIR PATRIOTISM.

THE STORIES IN THIS BOOK ARE PERSONAL AND FOR REAL. THEY CONVEY VIVIDLY AND DRAMATICALLY WHAT EVERY CREW WAS UP AGAINST IN THE DARK SKIES OVER GERMANY. FLAK, SEARCH-LIGHTS, NIGHT FIGHTERS, COLLISIONS, TECHNICAL FAILURE, WEATHER – ALL HAZARDS THAT HAD TO BE FACED, ENDURED AND OVERCOME, WITH THE ODDS STACKED AGAINST THE CREWS ON EVERY SUCCEEDING FLIGHT AS THEY DOGGEDLY PRESSED ON TO THE MAGIC NUMBER OF THIRTY TRIPS, WHICH SIGNIFIED THE COMPLETION OF THEIR FIRST TOUR. THE TALES BRING HOME TO THE GENERATIONS THAT FOLLOWED THE SUPREME COURAGE, THE PROFESSIONAL COMMITMENT AND THE DEDICATED ENDURANCE OF THE YOUNG AIRCREW OF THE BOMBER SQUADRONS IN THEIR TASK TO GAIN FINAL VICTORY AND RETAIN OUR FREEDOM.

BOMBER COMMAND'S WORST NIGHT WAS ON 30/31 MARCH 1944, WHEN AN ATTACK ON NUREMBERG WITH 795 BOMBERS WENT HORRIBLY WRONG: 95 AIRCRAFT AND 665 TRAINED AIRMEN WERE SHOT DOWN IN A FEW HOURS. MORE AIRCREW WERE LOST IN THAT ONE NIGHT THAN FIGHTER COMMAND LOST IN THE FOUR MONTHS OF THE BATTLE OF BRITAIN!

HOW DID THE YOUNG AIRMEN COPE WITH THEIR STRANGE LIFE? LIVING ON WARTIME AIRFIELDS IN DRAUGHTY, DAMP NISSEN HUTS WITH PRIMITIVE ABLUTIONS AND WASHING FACILITIES; MUD EVERYWHERE IN WINTER; DISPERSAL GONE MAD, WITH LIVING QUARTERS, MESSES, FLIGHT OFFICES AND AIRCRAFT PARKING LOTS ALL HUNDREDS OF YARDS APART. ONE NIGHT IN THE PUB PLAYING DARTS WITH THE LOCALS OR DANCING WITH WAAFS IN THE NEAREST TOWN; THE NEXT HUNDREDS OF MILES DEEP INTO GERMANY TO FACE THE MOST FORMIDABLE AIR DEFENCES IN EUROPE. HOW DID THEY CONTINUE FLIGHT AFTER FLIGHT WHEN ON EACH TRIP THEY LEARNED MORE ABOUT THE DANGERS THAT FACED THEM AND WOKE IN THE MORNING WITH EMPTY BEDS IN THEIR HUT?

READ THESE STORIES AND REMEMBER YOU OWE YOUR PRESENT WAY OF LIFE AND ITS LUXURY, PROSPECTS AND SAFETY TO THAT GENERATION, WHICH GAVE ITS ALL TO WIN THAT VICTORY, AND WHICH SAVED OUR FREEDOM TO LIVE OUR LIVES AS WE CHOOSE AND NOT UNDER SLAVERY.

**TONY IVESON, DFC, AE, CRAeS** ONE-TIME LANCASTER PILOT ON NO. 617 'THE DAMBUSTERS' SQUADRON, RAF BOMBER COMMAND. MAY 2011

# INTRODUCTION

WITH AN AVERAGE AGE OF JUST 22, THE YOUNG AIRMEN OF THE ROYAL AIR FORCE'S BOMBER COMMAND, ALL VOLUNTEERS, BEGAN OPERATING WITHIN MINUTES OF THE START OF THE SECOND WORLD WAR. CONTINUALLY, THROUGH TO MAY 1945, THE AIRCREWS, WITH THE ODDS HEAVILY AGAINST THEM, FOUGHT IN DEFIANCE OF NAZI AGGRESSION. THEY DEFENDED THE BRITISH ISLES AGAINST INVASION, THEY TOOK THE WAR DIRECTLY TO GERMANY, THEY SUPPORTED THE LAND CAMPAIGNS, THEY OPPOSED THE ENEMY NAVY AND U-BOAT THREATS, AND THEY COUNTERED THE GERMAN V-WEAPON OFFENSIVES. BUT THE COST WAS HIGH. FROM THIS MULTINATIONAL FORCE, INCLUDING BRITISH AIRMEN, CANADIANS, AUSTRALIANS, NEW ZEALANDERS, SOUTH AFRICANS, RHODESIANS, INDIANS, POLES, CZECHS, FRENCH, AMERICANS, NORWEGIANS, DUTCH, BELGIANS AND JAMAICANS, A STAGGERING 55,573 AIRMEN WOULD LOSE THEIR LIVES, 9,838 WOULD BECOME PRISONERS OF WAR AND A FURTHER 8,403 WOULD SUFFER WOUNDS.

FIGHTING HIGH PUBLISHING BRINGS TOGETHER NOTABLE MILITARY AVIATION AUTHORS TO TELL THE STORIES OF SOME OF THOSE WHO 'FAILED TO RETURN' FROM OPERATIONS. THE CAREFULLY SELECTED

## 125,000
APPROXIMATE NUMBER OF AIRCREW WHO SERVED WITH RAF BOMBER COMMAND DURING WWII

## 55,573
NUMBER OF AIRCREW WHO WERE KILLED WHILE SERVING WITH RAF BOMBER COMMAND

STORIES DEMONSTRATE THE DIVERSITY OF OPERATIONAL DUTIES UNDERTAKEN BY THE AIRCREWS, WHILE HIGHLIGHTING THE EXTREMES OF DANGER THEY FACED, OFTEN DAY AFTER DAY AND NIGHT AFTER NIGHT. MOST WOULD NOT SURVIVE THEIR ORDEAL; APPROXIMATELY HALF OF THE MEN WHO WERE LOST SERVING WITH BOMBER COMMAND HAVE NO KNOWN GRAVE. MANY OTHERS WOULD SEE OUT THE WAR INCARCERATED IN AN ENEMY POW CAMP.

THE AUTHORS, DRAWING UPON SURVIVING VETERAN ACCOUNTS, FAMILY ARCHIVES, OFFICIAL DOCUMENTS, WARTIME MEMOIRS AND LETTERS, FLYING LOGBOOKS, AND RELATIVE AND WITNESS RECOLLECTIONS, PIECE TOGETHER THE EXTRAORDINARY, GRIPPING, YET ULTIMATELY TRAGIC EVENTS SURROUNDING THE LOSSES DESCRIBED. *BOMBER COMMAND: FAILED TO RETURN* ENSURES THAT THE MEMORIES OF ALL THE YOUNG MEN, SOME WOULD EVEN SAY BOYS, WHO SACRIFICED ALL, ARE KEPT ALIVE.

'LEST WE FORGET.'

# 8,403

NUMBER OF AIRCREW WHO WERE WOUNDED
WHILE SERVING WITH RAF BOMBER COMMAND

# 9,838

NUMBER OF AIRCREW WHO BECAME PRISONERS
OF WAR

## CHAPTER ONE

# THE FIRST OF THE BEST

SEAN FEAST

THE MEN OF BOMBER COMMAND CAME FROM ALL WALKS OF LIFE. AT THE BEGINNING THEY WERE AN ASSORTMENT OF REGULARS, WEEKEND FLYERS AND MEMBERS OF THE ROYAL AIR FORCE VOLUNTEER RESERVE, ALL OF WHOM SHARED THE SAME DANGERS. FLAK AND FIGHTERS WERE NO RESPECTERS OF RANK, TITLE OR EVEN – ON OCCASION – EXPERIENCE. NOR WAS THE WEATHER. DEATH WAS A COMMON BOND. ONE OF THOSE EARLY BOMBER COMMAND PIONEERS WAS JIMMY MARKS, AND HIS LOSS AS A SQUADRON COMMANDER IN 1942 ON HIS SIXTY-EIGHTH OPERATION WAS A TREMENDOUS BLOW TO THE COMMAND AND TO HIS MEN. HIS SELFLESS ACT IN STAYING AT THE CONTROLS OF HIS AIRCRAFT TO ALLOW OTHERS TIME TO ESCAPE MIGHT HAVE BEEN RECOGNIZED WITH A HIGHER AWARD. AS IT WAS, HE WAS TO RECEIVE IMMORTALITY IN THE RANKS OF THE BOMBER COMMAND 'GREATS'.

James Hardy Marks, Jimmy to his friends, was a deserved legend in the annals of Bomber Command. A tall, fair-haired and well-built young man, Jimmy lived in Sawbridgeworth on the Hertfordshire/Essex border from the age of 2. He attended Fawbert and Barnard Primary School in Old Harlow and then Newport Free Grammar School in Saffron Walden, where he excelled at cricket and football.

Like many young men of that era, he was passionate about aeroplanes and learned to fly with Brooklands Aviation in Sywell. Under the tutelage of a Flying Officer Grieve, he took his first flight in a ubiquitous DH82 Tiger Moth on 9 March 1937 and, three weeks later, after less than twelve hours' flying time, flew his first solo. On completion of his flying training in May 1937, he was assessed by the Chief Flying Instructor (CFI) as an 'average' pilot. His proficiency in the air would soon rapidly improve.

Formally commissioned into the Royal Air Force on 9 May 1937, Jimmy soon exchanged the rather antiquated Tiger Moth for the more modern Hawker Hart and Hawker Audax biplanes with No. 10 Flying Training School (FTS) at RAF Tern Hill. Still rated 'average', his flying was also deemed 'inaccurate' by the Officer Commanding. It did not prevent the young acting Pilot Officer from graduating, however, and in December 1937 he received orders to report to No. 77 (Bomber) Squadron at RAF Honington.

The Squadron, which had been disbanded at the end of the First World War, had only recently been re-formed, as the RAF sought to expand its bomber force under a new command after nearly two decades of stagnation. Jimmy originally flew the Audax, an aircraft with which he was familiar from the FTS, but then had to convert to the much larger Vickers Wellesley, whose arrival coincided with his own. The Wellesley was a single-engine monoplane bomber that was the first to make use of the geodetic design made famous subsequently by the Vickers Wellington. He was soon in the air, initially as second pilot and then taking the controls alone, making primarily local flights. Among his contemporaries at this time was a young sergeant pilot T. G. 'Hamish' Mahaddie, whose name would later become synonymous with the Pathfinder

Force and who ended the war as Group Captain T. G. Mahaddie, DSO, DFC, AFC.

This was still in the halcyon days of air force flying, and one of Marks's more pleasant duties was taking part in the Empire Day air display at Martlesham Heath in May 1938. By now, of course, there were whispers of a new war in Europe: Neville Chamberlain, the British Prime Minister, returned from talks in Munich in September 1938 to declare famously 'peace in our time', only to see the Germans invade the Sudetenland twenty-four hours later and the countdown to a new conflict start in earnest. At much the same time, No. 77 Squadron began receiving the first of its Armstrong Whitworth Whitley III twin-engine bombers – a comparatively long-range aircraft with which it would ultimately go to war.

**Below** Jimmy Marks, late 1939/early 1940. *(All images courtesy of The Pathfinder Museum, RAF Wyton).*

**Right**
Jimmy Marks in full
flying kit 1940/41.

**Right**
Jimmy Marks in full
flying kit 1940/41.

Jimmy began converting to the new aircraft almost immediately, making local and cross-country flights from his new base (RAF Driffield) as well as practising forced landings on one engine. By the time war was finally declared, he had clocked up more than forty hours on the type.

The honour, if that is the word, of conducting the first air operations fell to ten aircraft of No. 51 and No. 58 Squadrons, dropping more than six million leaflets (13 tons) on Hamburg, Bremen and the Ruhr. These two squadrons, along with Nos 10, 77, 78 and 102, went to make up No .4 Group head-quartered in Yorkshire. They all operated various different marks of Whitley, which, as the slowest of the heavier bombers at that time (against the Wellington and Handley Page Hampdens), were restricted to night operations.

Jimmy's turn came on the night of 5/6 September (in Whitley K8961), when he set off as second pilot to Flying Officer Gordon Raphael to conduct similar operations (leaflet raids were later to be given their own codename – 'Nickels'), but

soon after they were recalled. He had more luck two nights later, although on their return, and low on fuel, they were obliged to make a forced landing at a French airfield, smashing into a parked French Dewoitine 520 fighter that they had failed to see in the mist. Jimmy, Raphael and the three remaining crew were obliged to return by the boat train.

October was a comparatively quiet month. The first of the newer and more powerful Whitley Vs had started to arrive, but the Squadron had also suffered its first casualties. Whitley K8947, flown by Flying Officer Roland Williams, failed to return from a Nickel on the night of 15/16 October; the pilot lost his life, and the rest of his crew was captured. A little over a week later, N1358, a Whitley V, also failed to return, its pilot (Pilot Officer Philip Walker) and the entire crew being killed.

On 1 November, Jimmy and Gordon Raphael flew to RAF Dishforth for an inspection by His Majesty the King and various 'brass hats', among the more notable being Sir Cyril Newall, the Chief of Air Staff, and Sir Hugh Dowding of Fighter

Command fame. The Squadron was operating again on the night of 10/11, losing another Whitley V (N1364), skippered by one of most experienced officers and Jimmy's flight commander, Squadron Leader James Begg. No one survived from the crew of five.

There was little by way of air operations for the next four months as the whole of Europe was gripped by bitterly cold weather. Indeed it was the weather, rather than flak or fighters, that still represented the bomber crews' greatest danger, and an enemy more likely to result in their demise. Of the few sorties undertaken by the Squadron, nearly all comprised Nickels or reconnaissance, including a number of deep penetration raids to Poland, Czechoslovakia and beyond. Flying Officer J. H. Marks was mentioned in a dispatch from Air Chief Marshal Sir Edgar Ludlow Hewitt (Commander-in-Chief Bomber Command) on 20 January 1940 'for gallant and distinguished services'.

The lull known as 'The Phoney War' that had followed the Germans' Blitzkrieg of Poland was about to end, but there was still one important show to play. On 9 April, without warning, the German war machine rolled into Denmark and Norway, and the Squadron soon found itself in the thick of the action. Flying Officer George Saddington was shot down and killed looking for enemy shipping on the night of 11/12 April, and in the daylight hours that followed Jimmy took part in a formation search for the downed crew over the North Sea. Their search was in vain. On the 15th, they flew to Kinloss, with the intention of establishing a base from which they could mount operations against the airfields at Sola (Stavanger) and Vaernes (Trondheim) – the latter being at the extreme range for a heavy bomber at that time. The whole might of Bomber Command's night-bombing force was now concentrated on the German-held airfields.

Jimmy, as second pilot again to Gordon Raphael, attacked Trondheim on 16 April, encountering heavy flak but having the satisfaction of

**Left**
Whitley with a Halifax behind, circa July 1941.

13

seeing his bombs destroying a number of aircraft.
They went back to Trondheim again two nights
later, and had a nasty moment on their return
when an intercom lead jammed in the ailerons.
They also arrived home with less than five minutes
worth of fuel remaining in the starboard motor.
They were indeed lucky; Pilot Officer Ronald Hall,
on the same raid, was not. Short of fuel, he was
obliged to ditch in the sea and was killed in the
attempt. His crew, however, survived.

Jimmy was captain of his own aircraft for a raid
on the airfield at Fornebu (Oslo) on 1 May, with
Pilot Officer William Timoney in the co-pilot's
seat. Although they successfully dropped their
bombs and incendiaries on the target, they met
fierce resistance, Jimmy making note of more than
thirty searchlights and intense anti-aircraft fire.
Their aircraft (Whitley N1410) was hit on the
starboard leading edge, making for a long, uncomfortable journey home. It was a few days later that
the damage was repaired, such that Jimmy could

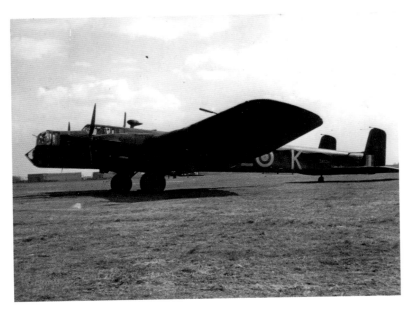

make the return trip from Kinloss to base, in the
company of the Squadron's Commanding Officer,
Wing Commander Charles Appleton.

This was Jimmy's last attack of the Scandi-
navian 'misadventure' – as it has come to be known
in the official history – the dress rehearsal before
the main event. On 10 May, the German army
finally made its move, and there followed an intense

period of operations that thrust 4 Group and No. 77
Squadron into the fray virtually without rest.
Jimmy, with his co-pilot Timoney, attacked a bridge
and road junction on the 11th, a crossroads on the
14th, and an oil refinery on the 18th. He reported
seeing 'the whole of Holland ablaze', and increasingly heavy opposition from the German defenders.
On the 20th he took Timoney, Sergeant Tindall
(the observer) and two wireless operator/air
gunners (Wop/AGs), Aircraftman Lucas and Aircraftman Pacey, to attack a bridge with 6 x 250lb
and 2 x 500lb bombs. Coned by searchlights from
the French (sic) and Germans, their Whitley (N1368)
suffered a direct hit, which disabled their hydraulic
system. The subsequent landing was made without
flaps but was otherwise uneventful. With the same
crew he returned from Cologne the following night
on just the one engine.

The month of May was a bloody time for the
Squadron: it lost a good many aircraft, pilots and
crews, although nothing compared to the losses of
the Fairey Battle Squadrons, which found themselves all but wiped out. Jimmy's erstwhile Captain,
Gordon Raphael, nearly came to grief on 18/19
May, when his aircraft was attacked and damaged
by a Messerschmitt Bf110, which was promptly shot
down by one of his gunners. Raphael was obliged
to ditch but was later rescued. (Gordon Raphael
would later go on to become a successful nightfighter pilot, winning the DSO, DFC and Bar and
becoming Officer Commanding No. 85 Squadron
before losing his life in a flying accident.)

June was no less hectic – a word that appears
more than once in Jimmy's logbook. Trips to the
Ruhr and Fleury were punctuated by various

testing flights at Farnborough and Boscombe Down with the new Squadron CO, Wing Commander J. MacDonald. (MacDonald had assumed command from Appleton that month.)

A distinct change of target came on 11 June, the day after the Italians had thrown in their lot with the Führer and declared war on Britain. An attacking force of 36 Whitleys flew to the airfields on Jersey and Guernsey to refuel, prior to the long haul over the Alps to Turin. The gesture demanded by British Prime Minsister Winston Churchill so nearly ended in disaster. Of the eight No. 77 Squadron aircraft involved, only one claimed to have bombed the target. Six, including Whitley N1365 flown by Jimmy Marks, were forced to abort, and one failed to return. Severe weather conditions, including electrical storms, caused both of Jimmy's engines to fail, and only his experience as a pilot – and a large slice of luck – saved the day.

Jimmy's 'press-on' attitude had not gone unnoticed by his superiors. The award of the Distinguished Flying Cross was strongly supported by the AOC No. 4 Group, Arthur 'Mary' Coningham. In the 'particulars of meritorious service', three separate raids (out of twenty-two operational flights then completed) are highlighted in which he pressed home his attacks with the utmost conviction. On two of these occasions, he remained over or near the target for more than an hour and a half because unfavourable weather conditions and poor visibility prevented him from ensuring accurate results.

In his memoirs (*Hamish: The Story of a Pathfinder*) Hamish Mahaddie recounts a similar example of Jimmy's eagerness to do the job properly. The Squadron was briefed to attack troop concentrations in a wood near Rotterdam. Jimmy suggested that, if they made a time-and-distance run from Rotterdam to the target, and then all dropped a flare, the aircraft that followed would be assured of accurate bombing. Mahaddie believes this was the first ever coordinated attempt to find a target, but despite the assurance of all the enthusiasts for the

**Left**
From Jimmy Marks's album. Nose art would become a common feature of Bomber Command aircraft throughout the war.

**Right**
From Jimmy Marks's album – the all-important ground crews at work.

scheme that the run was made with great care, not one of a dozen or more taking part in this unofficial experiment claimed to have seen one of the other's flares or Very lights. Jimmy, it should be noted, was undeterred by this initial failure, and tried again the following evening, with more promising results.

By now rated an 'exceptional' heavy bomber pilot and with more than 1,000 flying hours to his name, Jimmy was promoted to flight lieutenant in October 1940 and by April 1941 was flying with No. 58 Squadron (another 4 Group Whitley squadron) as a flight commander. His logbook tells of an exciting trip on 7 April when his Whitley was attacked over Emden. Air Marshal Sir Richard Peirse (the then C-in-C Bomber Command), in his Command routine orders, adds some detail:

The Captain was just about to bomb when he was attacked from the rear by a nightfighter; the first burst hit the starboard engine, which stopped, thereby immobilising the rear turret. A second attack from below would have had far more serious

consequences but for the protection offered by the 500lb bombs. On its final attack from head-on, the nightfighter approached so close that it is presumed that it must have struck the rudder of the Whitley with its wing. Half of the rudder was severed completely, and when last seen, the fighter was banking over steeply in a dive as though one wing was damaged.

At this time, in spite of jettisoning bombs, the aircraft had lost height to 700 feet, and the Captain decided to make for Norfolk, and at this height, limped across some 50 miles of hostile and occupied territory. The air observer pulled up the floorboards and discovered one 500lb bomb, which had not dropped. This he released by hand, after which the aircraft climbed gradually to 1,000 feet and a successful landing was made at Bircham Newton.

Jimmy's efforts were soon after recognized with his first Distinguished Service Order in July 1941 (officially gazetted on 23 September 1941), at which point he is credited with having completed fifty-two operations. As a flight commander, he is noted for 'his powers of leadership, enthusiasm and ability to carry out his job under any conditions'.

Over the next nine months, Jimmy flew only a handful of sorties. This did not mean, however, that he was in any way 'resting'. The Handley Page Halifax – the second of the four-engine 'heavies' – was now coming into service, and the first Whitley crews were being rapidly converted using the precious handful of aircraft then available. The first unit to receive the new aircraft was No. 35 Squadron, and it was under their tutelage that Jimmy learned to tame the new beast. With Squadron Leader Bradley at the controls, Jimmy undertook some local dual instruction on 27 July (in Halifax L9509) before taking the controls alone for himself later the same day to practise landings. In less than a fortnight he was back on operations, attacking Krupps on 7 August and Berlin five days later. He was again rated as an 'exceptional' heavy

bomber pilot and pilot-navigator by the No. 35 Squadron Commanding Officer, Wing Commander Basil Robinson.

Promotions tended to follow rapidly in Bomber Command at this time. Towards the end of December, Jimmy was promoted to squadron leader and three months later on 12 March was appointed to replace Robinson as Commanding Officer of No. 35 Squadron in the rank of wing commander. From every account given about their new CO from the aircrew who served with him, Jimmy threw himself into his new command with great gusto. The great German battleship, *Tirpitz*, was a favourite target of the time, lurking in the fjords around Trondheim. It was familiar territory and a familiar routine to some of the more veteran crews: the aircraft would first head north to Kinloss to shorten the distance before making the long and arduous journey across the North Sea to Norway.

The attack on 30 March, so meticulously planned, ended in total failure and the loss of three No. 35 Squadron crews. The same routine was

**Left** Jimmy Marks (front row, left) as a Flying Officer, with the DFC, circa June 1940, No. 77 Squadron.

**Right**
Jimmy Marks as
Commanding Officer
No. 35 Squadron,
1942.

repeated the following month (27 April), with the aircraft this time loaded with anti-submarine mines designed to detonate at a depth of 30 feet. Finding the target obscured by a smokescreen, Jimmy pressed home his attack from 150 feet. Sadly, the great monster was again unscathed, and the raid is noteworthy primarily for the loss of Halifax W1041 piloted by Wing Commander Donald Bennett, the CO of No. 10 Squadron. Bennett managed to evade capture, and shortly after his return to England was promoted to create and command the Pathfinder Force.

The raid was also noteworthy since it formed the main context for the award of a Bar to Jimmy's first DFC, an award that was subsequently elevated in importance to a Bar to his DSO on the recommendation of the new AOC No. 4 Group, Roddy Carr.

Jimmy led his Squadron on three of the famous 1,000 bomber raids: Cologne (30/31 May), Essen (1/2 June) and Bremen (25/26 June). For the last raid he took with him as an observer Group Captain John Whitley, the Station Commander at RAF Linton-on-Ouse, and a man never to shirk danger or responsibility.

He had further distinguished company, including his AOC, for an intriguing flight described in his log book simply as: 'To Radlett and return'. Radlett was the home of Handley Page, and for some time Jimmy had been looking at ways of improving the Halifax's performance. He had, on his own initiative, removed the front turret of his personal aircraft and replaced it with a modified wooden nose, covered in fabric and doped. The net result was an aircraft that was faster, could climb more quickly and had better fuel consumption than any other aircraft on the Squadron. (Handley Page later modified a number of Halifax aircraft with a faired nose for use with the long-range special duties squadron.)

In August 1942, shortly after Jimmy's 23rd birthday, No. 35 Squadron become one of the first units designated as part of Pathfinder Force, necessitating a move from Linton to RAF Graveley in Cambridgeshire, much closer to his family in Hertfordshire. It was a happy move for Jimmy, allowing him to jump into the station 'hack' and fly

to Sawbridgeworth to see his parents.

Within days of the move the Squadron was operating, taking part in the first ever Pathfinder Force-led attack. Sadly it was an unmitigated failure. The weather and winds were contrary to those forecasted, and the nearest bombs fell some 20 or so miles away.

There was a chance for the Squadon to redeem itself on 19 September, when the target was Saarbrücken; this was a relatively modest raid involving 118 aircraft. The crew of Halifax W7657 coded 'L' comprised Wing Commander Marks in the pilot's seat, navigator Flight Lieutenant Alan Child, DFC, wireless operator Pilot Officer Reginald Sawyer, DFM, mid-upper gunner Flight Lieutenant Norman Wright, and, in the rear turret, Pilot Officer Richard Leith Hay Clark. Child and Leith Hay Clark were their respective section leaders, both valuable men. The flight engineer was a young flight sergeant Bill Higgs:

Having carried out our night flying test (NFT) earlier in the day, we took off to attack Saarbrücken at 2001 hours and climbed steadily.

As far as I can remember we had a full moon – not the night to be flying over enemy territory. The sky was quite clear and we crossed over the channel and into France with no problems. During the flight towards Germany, I told the skipper that we were flying below a vapour trail. He looked up and said: 'No it's thin cloud'. Later, as we turned between Paris and Rheims I noticed that the 'thin cloud' seemed to be turning with us. I mentioned this to the skipper: 'You win,' he laughed, and told the gunners to keep an eye open for nightfighters.

When we neared the target, the luck went all the Germans' way. Thick mist appeared and when the navigator thought we were near the target, the skipper descended to 2,000ft and we carried out a square search for an hour. We could not see the ground and as target markers we were not allowed to drop our special marker incendiary bombs unless we could clearly identify the target. At that time we had no 'special equipment' to help us.

At this point I told the skipper that if we had to carry our bomb load home, we were going to have to leave soon or there wouldn't be enough fuel. The skipper immediately took the necessary action to leave the target area. As we climbed, I saw a Bf110 nightfighter flash past our starboard wingtip, nearly colliding with us. We levelled out at 11,000ft and passed out of Germany and into France. At 0030 hours I was calculating our fuel consumption when there was a sudden and tremendous explosion in the port wing. I stood up and looked out to see that our number five and six fuel tanks were on fire. The flames were going back beyond the rear turret.

At that point the aircraft dived and I hit the roof. We then pulled out of the dive and I crashed to the floor. I could see the skipper talking into his microphone but I could hear nothing through the intercom. The aircraft began falling again and once again my head hit the roof and I thought 'this is it'. The skipper once more managed to pull the aircraft out of the dive and I moved alongside him. He pointed to where Alan (the navigator) had opened the escape hatch. I went back to my position, clipped on my parachute and moved to the hatch.

It is amazing what strange thoughts pass through one's mind at a time like this. I looked at the opening and the small area of metal around it. I sat on the edge of the hatch and tried to drop through. Unfortunately the adjusting buckles on my parachute harness just happened to stick out above my shoulders and caught in the rim of the hatch. So there I was – half in, half out – stuck! Then I fell, and I remember the tail wheel making a dreadful noise as I flashed past it.

My parachute opened with a sharp 'crack' as soon as I pulled the ripcord and I breathed a sigh of relief. I saw the nightfighter approaching me and screwed my body into a ball to make it as small a target as possible. He didn't see me and turned his attentions to the burning Halifax. Shortly afterwards dear old 'L' hit the ground and exploded in a great mass of flames.

The aircraft crashed at Blesme, 11 kilometres east of Vitry Le François, with Jimmy Marks still at the controls. Alan Child and Richard Leith Hay Clark were killed with him. The Halifax was probably the victim of Leutnant Ferdinand Christiner of 4 Gruppe/Nachtjagdgeschwader 4 (4/NJG4), who claimed a Halifax shot down near Blesme at much the same time.

Jimmy's mortal remains and those of his navigator and rear gunner were eventually interred at the Choloy War Cemetery in France. Fifty years later, a memorial to the crew was unveiled at Blesme, and on 19 September 2004 a plaque commemorating Jimmy was unveiled by his sister in Sawbridgeworth's Memorial Hall.

Shortly after his death, Donald Bennett wrote to Jimmy's parents, enclosing a Pathfinder 'eagle' – the official badge of the Pathfinder Force – and the award certificate dated 19 September, the day he went missing. Bennett was in no doubt of Jimmy's qualities, describing him as 'one of the finest officers in the Service'. Bill Higgs is similarly not in any doubt. He owes his life to Jimmy Marks, the original Pathfinder:

None of us would have survived if it had not been for the skill and bravery of our pilot, Jimmy Marks. He was just about to be promoted to group captain and this was to be his last operational flight. How cruel can fate be? ●

## CHAPTER TWO

# THE MYSTERIOUS PHOENIX OF PAWLETT HAMS

### JULIAN EVAN-HART

FROM THE EARLY STAGES OF THE SECOND WORLD WAR THE ROYAL AIR FORCE DECIDED THAT AN INTERMEDIATE STAGE OF DEVELOPMENT WAS REQUIRED BETWEEN BASIC TRAINING AND OPERATIONAL DUTIES. THIS SO-CALLED INTERMEDIATE STAGE DEVELOPED INTO THE ORGANIZATION OF OPERATIONAL TRAINING UNITS (OTUs). THESE TRAINING UNITS CAN OFTEN APPEAR A RATHER NEGLECTED AREA OF AVIATION HISTORY, ALTHOUGH THIS IS IMPROVING WITH RESEARCH IN RECENT YEARS. OTUs WERE A VITAL TRANSITION STAGE IN THE TRAINING MATRIX OF FUTURE RAF BOMBER COMMAND CREWS AMONG OTHERS AND SUFFERED A HUGE AMOUNT OF LOSSES, NOT ONLY BECAUSE OF THE DEMANDS PLACED ON THEM AND THE ENSUING ACCIDENTS, BUT ALSO BECAUSE THEY HAD RATHER WAR-WEARY AIRCRAFT TO OPERATE WITH. THE INEXPERI-ENCE OF THESE TRAINING CREWS ALSO CONTRIBUTED TO THESE LOSSES, AS DID THE LUFTWAFFE'S NIGHTFIGHTER INTRUDER OPERATIONS, WHOSE EXPERIENCED PILOTS SOON FOUND OTU CREWS EASY PICKINGS IN THE DARK SKIES OF BRITAIN.

As the RAF's bomber offensive against Germany escalated, the OTUs were under constant pressure to train and release new crews. The following account relates to the crash of a No. 13 OTU Bristol Blenheim R3912 and the loss of its crew in the summer of 1942. No. 13 OTU had been formed at RAF Bicester on 8 April 1940 within No. 6 Group and comprised Nos 104 and 108 Squadrons equipped with Blenheims and Avro Ansons. Training initially began for daylight operations, but this was later extended to include night-intruder training. On 11 May 1942 No. 13 OTU was transferred to No. 92 Group. Many of

tragic or important; had they survived, who knows what their individual destinies and achievements might later have been. This is their story.

On the morning of 5 July 1942 three aircrew walked across the breeze-swept grass surface of RAF Bicester airfield towards the aeroplane they were scheduled to fly that day: 20-year-old Sergeant James Falconer Anderson (pilot), 33-year-old Sergeant Adam Hogg (observer) and 21-year-old Sergeant Gilbert Ingram McBoyle (wireless operator and gunner). The brief that morning had been nothing out of the ordinary for these men: a cross-country training flight, culminating in a

**Left** From left to right Adam Hogg, James Anderson, Gilbert McBoyle. *(Dave King, via relatives of Adam Hogg).*

the Bomber Command crews who later flew the 'Heavies' into the dark skies of the Reich would have had their basic training skills enhanced at the controls of an Anson or a Blenheim. Just one of these many losses will be examined here – resulting all too familiarly in the tragic and violent deaths of three airmen, all killed before they had had a chance to become operationally effective in the war effort. They were not destined to die in the flak-infested skies over a major German city, nor even to survive as POWs. Their loss is, however, no less

medium-level practice bombing session. As they got nearer to their rather weary-looking Blenheim, they noticed the glistening and running streaks of the cool night-time dew that was evident all over its paintwork. Climbing in, the crew could feel that the morning sun had already warmed the interior of their bomber, emphasizing its familiar pungent odour of old leather, oil and paint. The time was approximately 0930 hours and, after a few checks, the large radial Bristol Mercury engines coughed, whined and spluttered into life. They trundled and bounced down the grass runway, the tail lifted, and at 0950 hours they were airborne, briefly joining several pairs of buzzards that drifted lazily over the airfield. The weather was quite clear: mostly blue skies with occasional interrupted cloud layers at 3,000 feet and above and visibility subject to a typical summer haze. Heading on a westward flight path, they crossed England's countryside: a patch-work quilt of green meadows and yellow ripening wheat fields. Thousands of feet below it was perhaps only the 'dedicated' schoolboy who now glanced upwards to look, so familiar were aero engines in the crowded wartime skies. For the bombing practice, the Blenheim carried a series of 11lb practice bombs. Shaped like the elongated bombs from the previous war, these small missiles impacted on the ground, pressing in a detonation cap that fired a small charge, creating thick explosions of various coloured smoke. The smoke, of course, acted as a marker, making it easier for aircrews to establish the accuracy they had achieved. The continuous steady drone and vibration of the engines were constant companions for our aircrew, as they continued further on, making minor

navigational modifications. A final adjustment was required to bring them into line with the designated target practice site. In this instance this was a large brick-built cross positioned in a grass field a little distance away from Pawlett Hams Balloon Hangar. Pawlett itself is close to Bristol, and the Balloon Hanger is situated at the junction of Ham Road and Gaunts Road. The hangar survives to this day and is an immense structure, clad in corrugated iron sheets. At the time it was used for barrage-balloon training and cable-cutting tests and its huge size was to avoid the need to deflate the balloons when they were winched to the ground.

Climbing to an altitude of some 5,000 feet, the crew circled the site and observed the cross in the field. It was just before 1220 hours; the crew had been in the air for around two and a half hours. Flying to one side, they commenced the dive and were lost to sight as they entered a large section of white cloud layer. They reappeared releasing a cluster of bombs right over the target area. A series of sharp 'cracks' were heard as each bomb penetrated the hard soil and then produced a puff of thick creamy white smoke. As the smoke cleared,

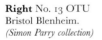

**Right** No. 13 OTU Bristol Blenheim. *(Simon Parry collection)*

the battered and twisted steel tail sections of the little bombs lay all over the grass around the target. The aircraft pulled up out of its dive, levelled off for a split second and commenced another dive. Initially there was nothing to alarm the eyewitness watching below, until the aeroplane entered that stage of progress 'where one realises that it ain't pullin' out of that'. Onlookers stood aghast as the bomber, now almost vertical, plummeted to earth.

The Blenheim's engines began to make a dreadful whining scream as the dive progressed. What had gone wrong? Had some catastrophic structural failure caused the second dive? Perhaps a bird strike, or was this simply a case of pilot error? Could there have been a collision with another aeroplane, hidden from view deep in the cloud layer? Or, as some would later suggest, had this unfortunate crew flown into a balloon cable from the nearby installation? Inside the cramped confines of the Blenheim one can but imagine the terror as the tremendous forces exerted themselves on crew and plane alike: the roar of the engines and the creaking of the airframe due to stress, loose objects falling past the crew to clatter against the glazed front cockpit panels, the view far down below ever increasing in whirling detail yet blurred with fear.

The frontal area of the bomber then impacted on a meadow at Pawlett Hams on the east bank of the River Parrett some 4 miles north of Bridg-water, in an instant frosting, cracking and shattering the Plexiglas panels and contorting the canopy framework. The propeller bosses impacted on the sun-baked surface, driving the blades, still rotating fully, into the underlying softer soil and clay. Two yellow-tipped blades from each engine were ripped from their boss mountings. Accompanied through the air by chunks of grassy soil, several of these blades were flung a considerable distance away, while the remaining blades twisted like strips of ribbon as they were rammed ever deeper into the ground. Next the large radial Bristol engines were violently forced to a stop, as gear teeth were stripped away, casing cracked and cylinder pots and pistons torn from their mounts in a grind-ing burst of metal fragments and hot oil.

The heavier drive shafts and reduction gearings smashed free of the remaining sections of cylinder pots and crashed on deeper into the clay. The weight of the engines upon initial impact carried the mid-cockpit section and main spar with them, crushing, lacerating and smashing apart the bodies of the pilot and observer trapped inside. The wing sections were ripped off outboard of each engine and the power of the impact instantly buckled the fuselage. The mid-upper turret containing Gilbert McBoyle crashed through its mounting, killing the young gunner instantly, and then tore through the contorting fuselage towards the already buried cockpit area. The heavy Browning 0.303 machine guns were torn from their mounts, smashing backwards through flesh and metal. The riveted panels of the rear fuselage sections burst open and were torn apart into crumpled serrated edged strips, causing some of the tail plane to detach and be hurled several yards from the main impact point. The force of the impact rammed clay deep into almost every fissure of the heavy engine parts. The fuel tanks exploded and a mixture of combusting oil and fuel began to vitrify the surrounding clay. The heat was intense, and a yellow orange fireball rose up into the sky, which soon turned into a brown oily mushroom shape that drifted across the meadowland.

Several locals started to run across the fields towards the crash site, but it was obvious there was little they could do, and the fear of unexploded bombs kept them back at some distance. The occasional crack and pop could be heard above the roar of the flames as 0.303 ammunition began to explode in the intense heat. To a depth of some 12 feet lay the shattered remains of the two engines, steaming against the moist clay. The entire buried, jumbled and contorted mass of wreckage was burning furiously at the upper regions of the impact crater. The recovery crew arrived to deal with the incident and cleared up the entire large surface area of lying wreckage. Furthermore they had to recover whatever human remains they could; this they did with great care and diligence. A steel wire hawser was attached to the main spar section, but this was too deeply buried for it to be dislodged, so a section of wire was detached and left in situ. This may have given rise to the opinions expressed by some locals who later went to the crash scene that the aeroplane had been involved in an incident with a balloon cable.

**Main Image**
The yellow painted hydraulic and articulated technology of modern times reaches into the soil in a quest to recover the technology of a bygone aviation era.

**This page, clockwise from top**
Main undercarriage section with punctured but intact rubber tyre; first time above ground since 5th July 1942 a twisted propeller blade is examined after recovery.; another propeller blade, carefully lifted from over six feet down in the oil and carbon soaked clay.

**This page, clockwise from top** A mass of fused, once molten and exploded casings and bullet tips were taken away for safe disposal.; a small plaque of remembrance had been prepared for the occasion. At the end of the dig this plaque was presented to the landowner, Mr David Pusey; slightly twisted propeller blade still attached to the boss. *(All iamges Courtesy of Dave King)*

Once the recovery crew had achieved their aims, several parts of the aeroplane were unceremoniously dumped back into the crater, which was roughly back filled. Over the next few years the in-filled area settled, which created a noticeable depression, around which, if one looked carefully, several small twisted pieces of airframe were still evident in the grass. As the decades passed the event became part of local folklore: the crater was still there, but people who actually remembered why began to dwindle in number. No concern or interest was shown for over half a century, when in 1996 a certain Tim Hake started to do some research.

## One Man's Quest

Tim was keen on finding out as much as he could about the incident with a view to possibly excavating whatever remains of the aeroplane lay buried on site. Back in the winter of 1996 Tim was a member of the now defunct Somerset Aviation Enthusiasts Group and was looking for a new excavation project. A chance conversation with fellow member Colin Parish revealed that Colin and his father knew the field where the Blenheim was supposed to have come down. Having sought permission from Mr and Mrs David Pusey, the landowners, they all met a few days later below the Pawlett Balloon Hangar, and Tim was shown the field. After about half an hour they concentrated on a shallow depression visible in the suspected meadow. A brief metal detector survey around the depression revealed just a few minute pieces of airframe. Then a larger Whites Deep Seeking model detector was employed and showed high potential for significant quantities of buried wreckage. Later Tim traced a No. 13 OTU document relating to the crash, which stated that the engines were buried at about 12 feet in depth, and that any technical assessment of the reasons for the crash was impossible, as the airframe was so badly smashed. What was left? Tim was determined to find out – and he would need every ounce of that dedicated attitude. At about this time Tim met Dave King and Melvin Brownless, who kindly did much associated research, including the location of a photograph of the actual aircrew. Armed with as much information as possible, Tim then submitted an application for a licence to excavate the remains of Blenheim R3912. However, the application was refused on the grounds that there might still be practice bombs in the wreckage. Tim had to prove this was not the case, but a trip made to the then Public Records Office (now The National Archives), at Kew, London, to examine No. 13 OTU records revealed nothing. Mr and Mrs David Pusey the landowners were not amused at all: they had sublet the land; was there a risk to their tenant of exploding bombs? They drafted a letter, asking the Ministry of Defence to render the land safe, but this too was to no avail. Tim even suggested that the MOD itself recover the aeroplane and he would watch from a distance. The reply indicated that this might be possible, but that the remains, if any were recovered, would be scrapped.

Tim and his colleagues then joined the British Aviation Archaeological Council, which started to examine licence applications that had been refused on the grounds of practice ordnance still being present. The MOD finally agreed to reassess such cases. Incredibly a decade had passed since Tim's determined efforts had begun. Then one day it was announced that the dig could proceed so long as Squadron Leader A. Swann from the Explosive Ordnance Disposal (EOD) at Wittering could attend. At this point Gareth Jones, one of the UK's leading experts in Forster Magnetometer usage, was asked to survey the site. The conclusion was that at least one, if not two, engines and undercarriage assemblies were still present, with an assorted mass of wreckage in between. However, a further issue arose when the site at Pawlett was dedicated as a Site of Special Scientific Interest. An action plan outlining measures to restrict pollution, soil disturbance, and disturbance to ground-nesting birds and, in particular, newts was submitted to Natural England, and was accepted. July 2007 was the month scheduled to see what the crash site would reveal.

## The Excavation

So it was on 14 July 2007 a small group of individuals arrived at the meadow into which the Blenheim had fallen so long before, and were accompanied by a 13-ton tracked excavator. The site was marked out and the excavation commenced. The massive tooth-edged bucket began slicing easily through the rich top soil. At just a few inches depth, traces of rust and blue aluminium oxide (known as Daz to diggers) was evident. Metal detector surveys revealed numerous small targets.

The team decided to excavate above the biggest magnetometer reading and found the shattered remains of a Bristol Mercury engine, along with undercarriage legs and the remains of one wheel with tyre. The final fragments were recovered at a depth of a fraction over 12 feet. Evidence of extreme heat subjection via fire was visible everywhere, with much wreckage having been burnt. The excavation was widened to encompass the middle and the point where it was suspected that the second engine lay. This second power plant was also uncovered at a depth of 12 feet; it too was in a very smashed condition. In fact, just the crank shaft and supercharger fans remained together. Both propeller bosses were located, each having a single blade still in situ. A length of steel hawser wire could now be seen still attached to the remains of the main spar, left behind by the wartime recovery team. Throughout the excavation many manufacturers and data plates were located, as well as a substantial section of elevator. Poignantly, several burnt sections of parachute silk were recovered, clearly indicative that the crew went in with their aeroplane. Further evidence was discovered in the form of harness buckles and several coins. These artefacts were recovered among many exploded rounds of ammunition, many still in the remains of the two large aluminium feed boxes for the top turret. This is particularly interesting, as the area of discovery makes it almost certain that these buckles and coins once belonged to the gunner Sergeant McBoyle. Large sections of compressed skinning were also unearthed, including several that bore repairs and flak patches. This evidence clearly points out that R3912 had seen combat action before and was perhaps rather 'war weary' by the time No. 13 OTU received her. In total, some three

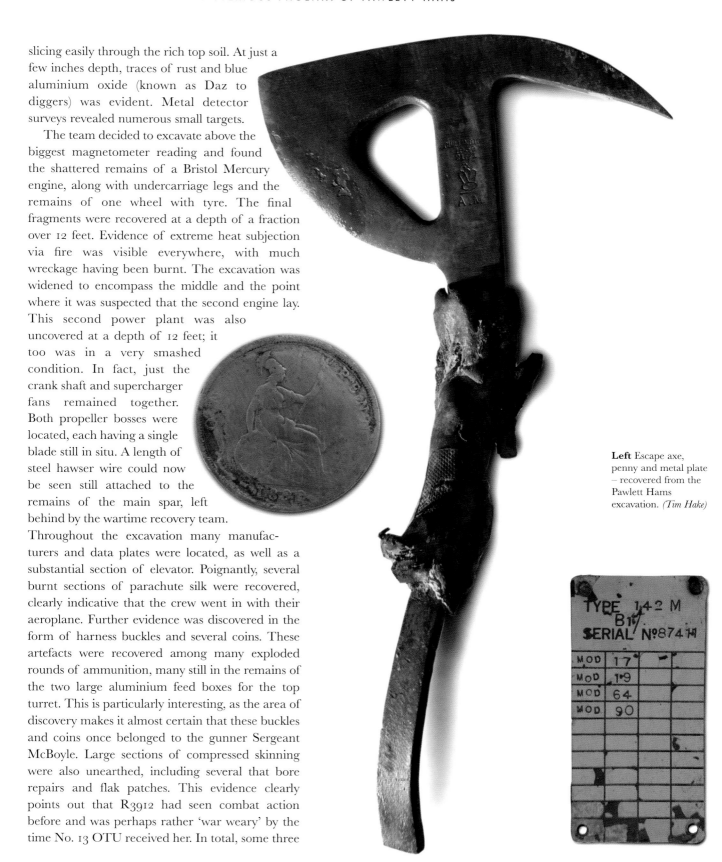

**Left** Escape axe, penny and metal plate – recovered from the Pawlett Hams excavation. *(Tim Hake)*

LUBRICATION INSTRUCTION

AT INSTALLATION
CAM LUBRICATING PAD 1 DROP.
REPEAT AT 40-HOUR INSPECTIONS.
USE OIL. WINTER GRADE
(STORES REF 34A/33)

ROTAX LTD
LONDON. N.W.10.

Parachute fabric,
lubrication instruc-
tions plate, piston and
metal disc – recovered
from the Pawlett
Hams excavation.
*(Tim Hake)*

FIT
1/ BOLT
C    G
DATUM

tons of wreckage were recovered from the crash site before the crater was back filled for the second time in sixty-five years. Later cleaning of the recovered artefacts incredibly brought about the discovery of flight maps, parts of the controls and even more sections of parachute silk.

## A Blenheim Rises from the Ashes and its Aircrew are Remembered

The excavation itself generated a lot of publicity. Local newspapers covered the event; it even made a feature in the *Sun* newspaper. The BBC came to film the wreckage and talk to Tim about the event. As a result of this publicity, Tim was approached by the Bristol Aero Collection, and he offered their representatives the opportunity of having any useable parts for their Bolingbroke restoration project. This offer was taken up, and several parts of Blenheim R3912 are now at the Bristol Aero Collection. This collection also now houses a propeller blade and hub, crank case and piston, the main undercarriage oleos, a cylinder and an oxygen cylinder, all on display at their Kemble Museum. The display is very tastefully arranged, with a photograph of the crew beside these artefacts reminding all who visit of their supreme sacrifice.

Research is still ongoing into the background of each crew member. It is difficult to undertake such work and not reflect on the lives of these young men: James Anderson the pilot, who was so young and youthful and yet was in charge of a bomber and its crew; Adam Hogg, the observer, who was just about to come home on leave and announce his engagement to a Miss Netta Wilson. Whatever became of Netta; how did her life work out after tragically losing her fiancé to be. Could she still be alive?

The marvels of such historical timelines combined with modern technical communications is emphasized by the fact that a relative of Sergeant Gilbert McBoyle was using the Internet to research a relative when a Google search revealed details associated with him. Via Simon Parry's superb website, www.redkitebooks.co.uk, this relative discovered the full story of what had happened. This is all the more remarkable, as until this point the family had known very little about their relative or this incident at all.

We will probably never know the exact reasons behind the deaths of these brave men, and therefore this factor still remains a mystery. If ever you visit or even just pass through Pawlett Hams, or you are standing just examining the impressive Balloon Hangar, as you look up in awe at the immense size, and as the wind rattles and clatters the orange-stained corroding corrugated cladding, please spare a thought for the three brave aircrew who died just a little distance from where you are. ●

### The crew of R3912

**Sergeant Gilbert Ingram McBoyle** 1178919, aged 20, of Fratton near Portsmouth was later laid to rest in Section C Grave 179 at the Bridgwater Cemetery in Quantock Road. He was the son of George Ingram and Hilda Kate McBoyle of Fratton near Portsmouth.

**Sergeant James Anderson** 591536, aged 21, was returned to Scotland and laid to rest in Edinkillie Parish Churchyard in Plot A.8 Grave 71.5. He was the son of James and Jean Falconer Anderson of Dunphail.

**Sergeant Adam Hogg** 1552074, aged 33, was laid to rest in the Hawick (Wellogate) Cemetery, Burghal Portion Grave 34. He was the son of Adam and Margaret Hogg of Hawick. Prior to joining the RAF, Adam Hogg had been a retail manager working for Messrs Innes, Henderson & Co. and was a keen participant in amateur dramatics.

**Far left** The grave of James Anderson at Edinkillie Parish Churchyard. *(Julie Munro)*

**Left** The grave of Gilbert McBoyle at Bridgwater (Quantock Road) Cemetery. *(Brian Bateman)*

## CHAPTER THREE

# THROUGH TRIALS TO THE STARS

## CHRISTOPHER YEOMAN

FOR MANY OF US TODAY THE MOST PROMINENT IMAGE WE HAVE OF THE BATTLE OF BRITAIN IS THAT OF HURRICANES AND SPITFIRES DUELLING WITH LUFTWAFFE BOMBERS AND MESSERSCHMITT FIGHTERS HIGH ABOVE BRITAIN IN VAPOUR-TRAILED SUMMER SKIES. IN CONTRAST, THE IMAGE OF RAF BOMBERS TAKING OFF INTO THOSE SAME SUMMER NIGHTS IS NOT ONE USUALLY ASSOCIATED WITH THAT MOST CRITICAL AND NOW HISTORIC AERIAL CONFLICT OF 1940. BETWEEN JULY AND THE END OF OCTOBER 1940, BOMBER COMMAND FLEW 9,180 SORTIES THAT UNDOUBTEDLY PROVED A HINDRANCE TO HITLER'S INVASION PREPARATIONS. BUT LIFE IN A BOMBER WAS UNFAVOURABLE AT BEST. UNLIKE AN RAF FIGHTER PILOT, A BOMBER CREW DID NOT HAVE THE ADVANTAGES OF SPEED, MANOEUVRABILITY, OR THE COMFORT OF FRIENDLY TERRITORY BENEATH THEIR WINGS. WITHOUT THE PROTECTION OF ESCORTING FIGHTERS, THOSE LONG, DARK TRIPS ACROSS THE ENGLISH CHANNEL WERE STRENUOUSLY TENSE AND RENOWNED FOR BEING EXCEPTIONALLY DANGEROUS. IT TOOK A TREMENDOUS AMOUNT OF COURAGE TO STEP INTO A BOMBER NIGHT AFTER NIGHT KNOWING THAT ANTI-AIRCRAFT FIRE, NIGHTFIGHTERS, MACHINE FAILURE AND DISORIENTATION COULD BE AWAITING THEM. SUCH WAS THE COURAGE FOUND ON-BOARD ARMSTRONG WHITWORTH WHITLEY T4171 DURING THE FINAL MONTH OF THE BATTLE OF BRITAIN.

O N A CLEAR DAY in July 2009, I visited Ship Lane Cemetery in Farnborough to find the gravestone of a relative whom I have never known. As I walked around the peaceful, well-kept grounds, I soon arrived at the burial site of Leonard F. P. Adlam. After resting a wild poppy flower at the headstone of the grave, I spent a quiet moment reflecting on his sacrifice. The headstone inscription told the tale of a widow who had lost her beloved husband when he was just 25 years of age. The endearing stone flower pot nearby bore a loving message from his only daughter, Delphine. Regrettably not uncommon for the time, another husband and father had been lost in 1940, in the service of his country during the Second World War.

Leonard Frank Percy Adlam was born on 26 July 1915, in Kent. In his youth Adlam attended the County School for Boys in Gillingham, where he developed into a thoroughly educated and athletic young man. In December 1931, his headmaster, Mr H. C. Barnard, wrote a glowing report that offers a splendid insight into Adlam's character:

He is a boy of outstanding ability, intelligent and conscientious. Last summer he sat for the London University School Certificate, in which he achieved an excellent result, reaching distinction standard in mathematics and matriculation, standard in

**Left**
Adlam's flying log-book.
*(Chris Yeoman)*

**Below**
Leonard Adlam's grave in 2009, Ship Lane Cemetery, Farnborough.
*(Chris Yeoman)*

English, history, geography, heat, light and sound, and chemistry… Adlam's character and conduct throughout his school career have been exemplary. On several occasions he was elected by his school fellows as Form Captain, and last September I appointed him a School Prefect, in which capacity he has shown an excellent sense of responsibility and power of control. He has also distinguished himself in several branches of sport, especially in cricket and rugby football… It is obvious, therefore, that he is an intelligent, thorough and reliable boy. I have considerable respect for his character and capabilities and can recommend him cordially and without reserve for any position for which these qualities are requisite.

In 1934, Leonard Adlam married Phyllis Elsie Yeoman, and on 11 February the following year they had a daughter, whom they named Delphine Adlam. After working at a bank and in the insurance business for some time, Adlam decided to join the Royal Air Force Volunteer Reserve, with hopes of becoming a pilot. In early 1939, his hopes were realized.

The very first entry in Adlam's flying logbook is dated 9 April 1939. It was on this date that one Flying Officer Townsend took a green passenger up in a De Havilland Tiger Moth aircraft to demonstrate the effects of the controls, handling of the engine and straight and level flying. The following

**Right** Leonard
Adlam, back row,
third from right.
*(Chris Yeoman)*

weeks at No. 16 Elementary and Reserve Flying
Training School, Adlam was kept busy with
classroom study and dual flying with various
instructors. After notching up over fifteen hours'
flying time, Adlam flew solo on 24 June 1939, in
Tiger Moth K4257.

In May 1940, Adlam had gained experience
flying Blackburn B-2 and Miles Master aircraft,
and while at No. 8 Flying Training School he was
rated as an 'above average' pilot. A month later,
while at No. 7 Operational Training Unit RAF
Hawarden, Adlam was given the opportunity to fly
an aircraft like no other: the Supermarine Spitfire.
Over a two-day period Adlam flew on seven
occasions in six different Spitfires; handling, cross
country and formation flying, followed by steep
turns and landings. By the end of this conversion
course, Adlam had flown 170 hours.

Up until this point, it appeared that Adlam was
being prepared to join a fighter squadron, but for
some reason, perhaps because of his age, he was
posted to No. 11 OTU to convert to bomber

aircraft. From 29 July to 7 September 1940, Adlam
spent his time flying Vickers Wellington aircraft.
Two days after his last flight in a Wellington MkI A,
Adlam's acquired bomber training was about to
be utilized.

On 9 September 1940, Sergeant Leonard Adlam
arrived at RAF Linton-on-Ouse in North Yorkshire
to join No. 58 Squadron, which proudly bore the
motto *Alis nocturnis* – 'On the wings of the night'.
The Squadron formed part of No. 4 Group in
Bomber Command and was equipped with
Armstrong Whitworth Whitley Mk V aircraft. The
Mk V was the most-produced version of the
Whitley; its modifications brought noticeable
improvements over previous versions of the aircraft.
The Whitley V was comparable to the Luftwaffe's
three 'heavy' bombers, but, although slightly slower,
it could carry a larger bomb load. The Mk V also
included a hydraulically operated rear turret that
was tightly sealed and armed with four machine
guns. The wings were also modified with de-icing
equipment and the tail was extended to improve

**Left**
Adlam , front row,
second from right,
at Advanced Flying
Training School at
Bassingbourne.
*(Delphine Hayes)*

the rear gunner's field of fire.

By the time Adlam arrived, No. 58 Squadron had already been actively involved in an impressive number of offensive raids, bombing industrial targets, usually in conjunction with No. 77 Squadron. Going back to the outset of war, it was in fact No. 58 and No. 51 Squadron Whitleys that were the first aircraft to penetrate Germany in the Second World War, when they performed a leaflet raid on 3/4 September 1939.

The day following Adlam's arrival, he was airborne as second pilot in Whitley P4991 on his first offensive raid of the war. Piloting the aircraft was Flying Officer Fleming, with Phillips, Haigh and Johnson making up the rest of the crew. The crew set off for Bremen at 2300 hours, but owing to heavy cloud they were unable to locate any targets and returned to base with a full bomb load at 0630 hours the next morning.

On 15 September 1940, Adlam, as second pilot, flew a night sortie in Whitley P4991 with Flying Officer Fleming and Sergeants Green, Haigh and

Hunter-Muskett. The crew were detailed to raid Hamburg, but the mission became a hair-raising experience for an unexpected reason and the aircraft was forced to jettison its bombs over the sea.

No. 58 Squadron's Operations Record Book explains why:

Proceeded from LINTON at time stated [19.50] for HAMBURG. Owing to icing of aircraft, aircraft got

**Left** Adlam, right,
at Brough, Scotland.
*(Delphine Hayes)*

Adlam, far left, at
RAF Linton-on-Ouse,
1940. *(Delphine Hayes)*

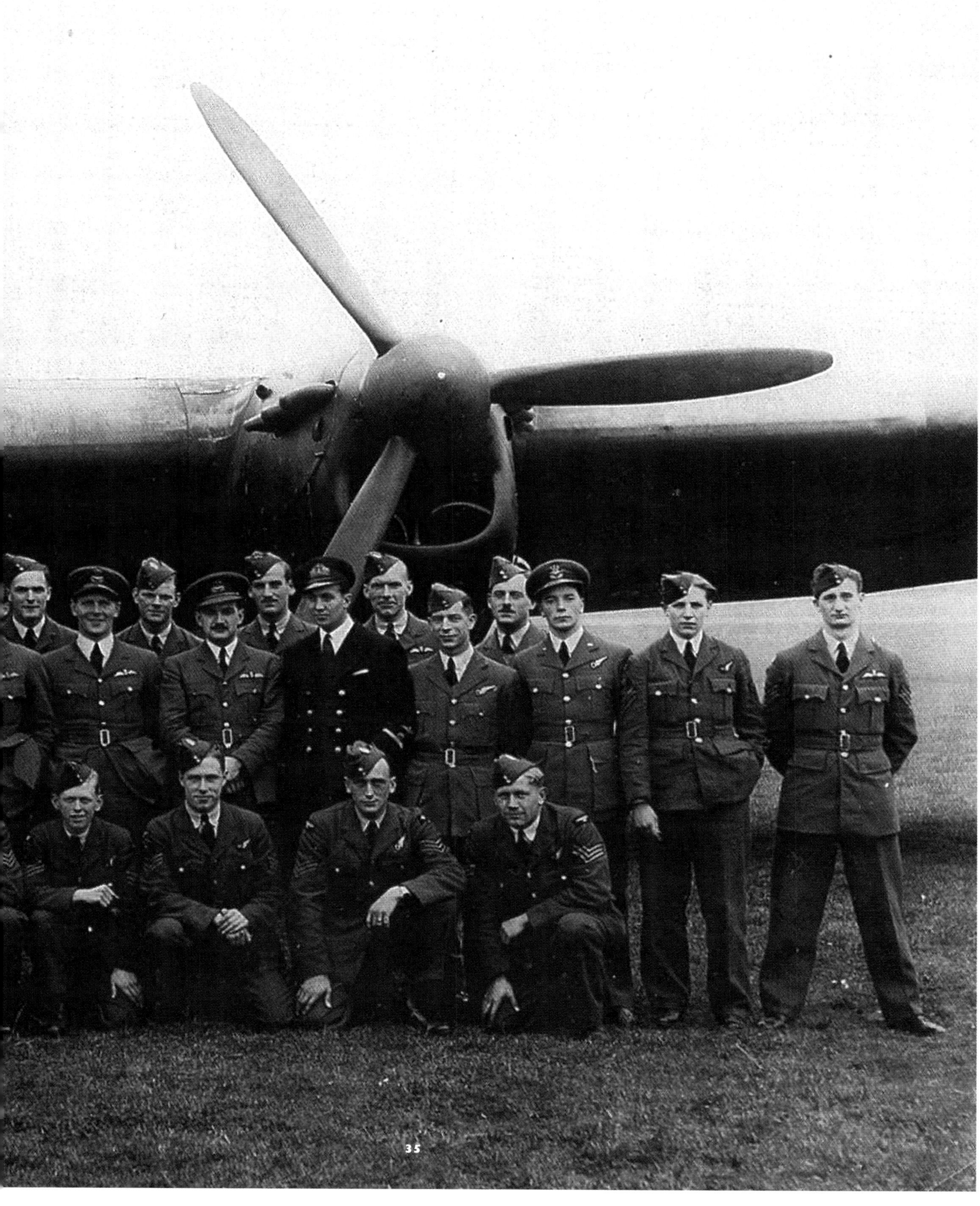

into a dive at 14,000 feet and could not be pulled up until 7,000 feet. Fabric and part of main plane carried away. Bombs were jettisoned at 'safe'. Aircraft returned and landed at LINTON at time stated. [00.20]

Eight days later, in Whitley T4174, Fleming and Adlam were once again deterred from reaching their target (Berlin), because of an unserviceable starboard engine. After only two hours and fifteen minutes in the air, they returned to base.

Thus far operations were proving to be frustrating and, on the night of 2/3 October, the difficulties would continue for the Squadron. Because of heavy cloud concealing the primary targets, the majority of the Squadron carried out attacks on secondary targets. Fleming and Adlam's Whitley made two level attacks from 9,000 feet but witnessed no results.

On Sunday 20 October 1940, Adlam accompanied Pilot Officer Ernest H. Brown in Whitley T4171 for an air test. After a fifteen-minute local flight, the pilots and crew found the aircraft suitable for the evening's operation. At 1900 hours the throaty growl of two Rolls Royce Merlin X engines sounded into the evening air at RAF Linton-on-Ouse. The unmistakeable sound, unlike any other, belonged to an Armstrong Whitworth Whitley V of No. 58 Squadron. As Pilot Officer Brown opened up the aircraft's throttles, the noise grew increasingly louder as it trundled across the grass aerodrome. In no time at all the Whitley, known as 'O for Orange' because of its code markings 'GE-O', was airborne and climbing into the open sky. It had already been an eventful day for the RAF, which was particularly busy in the south of England fending off Luftwaffe attackers. Over 300 sorties were flown by the enemy fighter-bomber pilots of Jafu 2 throughout the day, and at night their sorties continued, with London and Coventry being their main targets. With No. 58 Squadron Whitleys airborne, including O for Orange, it was now Bomber Command's turn to take the fight across the Channel.

With instructions to bomb the Skoda factory at Pilzen in Czechoslovakia, No. 58 Squadron

**Right** A damaged Whitley wing, possibly due to the incident of 15 September 1940. *(Delphine Hayes)*

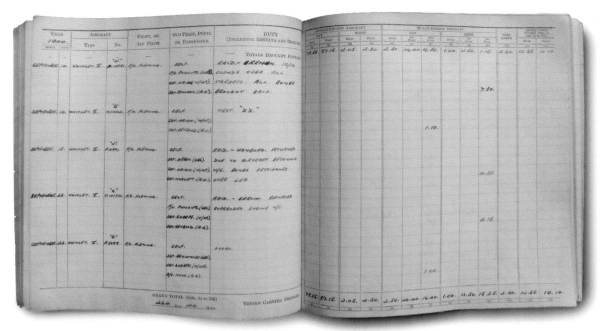

**Left** A look at the pages from Adlam's flying logbook. *(Chris Yeoman)*

navigated its way through the night sky. Pilot Officer Brown's crew consisted of Sergeant Leonard F. P. Adlam, who was the second pilot, Sergeant Robert E. Langfield, who was a wireless operator/air gunner, Sergeant Cyril S. G. Green, who was the observer, and Sergeant Marcel C. Caryll-Tilkin, who was also a wireless operator/air gunner. This last member of the five-man crew had already had a frightening ordeal just six weeks before this operation, when the aircraft he was in over Genoa ran out of fuel and was forced to ditch off the Margate coast. Fortunately, in the early hours of the morning Caryll-Tilkin and his crewmen were rescued from their dinghy.

When Pilot Officer Brown and his crew reached their intended target, they successfully bombed the Skoda factory, but not without paying a price. Enemy flak hit their aircraft, presumably causing damage to the port engine, as Pilot Officer Brown was hit by shrapnel and badly wounded. As he was unable to continue flying the aircraft, Sergeant Leonard Adlam took over the controls and turned their Whitley for home.

Feelings among the crew were undoubtedly tense, as the Whitley boys witnessed smoke trailing from the engine hit by flak, but Sergeant Adlam continued to fly the damaged aircraft across the Channel. Home seemed a long way off and the

cold dark water below most disturbing, but eventually the southern coast of England came into view and a small sense of relief was felt as Adlam flew the aircraft over friendly ground.

But as the Whitley limped further north it became lost and alarmingly short of fuel. With Pilot Officer Brown injured, the crew decided to head for base rather than abandon the aircraft and bale out. Adlam pressed on through the cloudy sky. Most likely strained and exhausted, the Whitley crew continued to work together in finding their way back to safety, but their beaten-up aircraft began to lose both height and fuel. Although on course for Linton-on-Ouse, the Whitley began rapidly to descend as it approached the Yorkshire Moors until finally O for Orange tragically crashed into a hillside at approximately 0612 hours on 21 October 1940. The crash was heard by nearby villagers, and soon after police, farmers and locals were hurrying towards the crash site.

Sadly, Pilot Officer Ernest Brown, Sergeant Leonard Adlam and Sergeant Marcel Caryll-Tilkin were killed. Sergeant Robert Langfield and Sergeant Cyril Green survived, although both were seriously injured. Indeed, Sergeant Green died in hospital two days later as a result of the serious nature of his internal injuries, leaving Sergeant Langfield as the sole survivor of the incident. At the

**Right** A photograph of Whitley T4171 taken sometime after the crash. *(Brian Rapier)*

**Below** A sketch of Whitley T4171. *(David Pritchard)*

time of the crash Langfield had been in the middle of the aircraft and had bent down to pick something up. He suffered major burns to his face and chest, a leg was smashed to bits and some of his ribs were broken. Despite his horrific injuries, Langfield dragged all but one of the crew out of the aircraft and when the rescue party arrived he was found unconscious, holding the hand of the airman who was trapped inside the burning Whitley.

The evidence suggested that the aircraft had crashed because of fuel shortage on its return from Czechoslovakia. Even the official Accident Records Card is believed to match this opinion, but a later development uncovered another insight into the crash when a German source stated that Whitley T4171 was claimed by a Luftwaffe Junkers Ju88 pilot.

The Ju88c pilot was Hauptmann Karl Hulshoff of I Gruppe, Nachtjagdgeschwader 2 (I/NJG2), who was over the north of England on a specialist intruder mission (one of the first of its kind). Catching sight of the smoking Whitley of No. 58 Squadron as it attempted to return to base, he apparently shot it down. Oddly enough, according to the Luftwaffe's combat records, Hulshoff claimed this aircraft as a 'Hereford', intercepted near Dishforth. (Hulshoff would rise to the rank of Oberstleutnant, with eleven credited victories to his name and is thought to have survived the war.)

Despite the contradicting records, the T4171 wreckage at Greenhow Moor denoted that an intense blaze had occurred to burn the aircraft out. With the aircraft reported as being out of petrol, it is unlikely that this was the cause of the fire; perhaps this was a consequence of falling victim to a Ju88 nightfighter. If, indeed, this was the case, then the loss of Brown, Adlam, Green and Caryll-Tilkin was even more tragic, considering all they had been

through previously on the night of the crash. They had succeeded in dropping their bombs on the Skoda armament factory and used all the initiative they could muster in getting their damaged aircraft back across the Channel to the English coast, and then, a short distance away from base with next to no fuel they were shot down by a lone Ju88 skulking like a predator through the North Yorkshire skies.

Aside from the loss of Adlam's Whitley, two additional aircraft were also lost on this operation but fortunately suffered no fatalities. One aircraft ditched in the River Humber and another ditched off Blakeney Point on the coast of Norfolk. Both crews were later rescued by lifeboat.

A day after the crash, a letter was written from No. 58 Squadron's Commanding Officer to Adlam's dear wife, Phyllis. Part of the letter read:

You will no doubt have received by now a notification of the death of your husband, 745662 Sgt. L. F. P. Adlam, from the Royal Air Force Records Office. You will no doubt wish for such details as I can give.

Your husband was a member of an aircrew returning from an operational flight in the early hours of the 21st October 1940. The aircraft crashed near Ingleby, Yorks and your husband, who was 2nd Pilot in the Aircraft, was killed

instantaneously. Three members of the crew of five were killed, and two received serious injuries.

I should like to take this opportunity of trying to express my deepest sympathy in your loss.

Shorty after this correspondence, Adlam's body was brought back to the south of England, and he was buried in Farnborough, Hampshire. A local newspaper at the time reported:

R.A.F. honours were accorded at the funeral of Sergt-Pilot L. F. P. Adlam, only son of Mr and Mrs F. Adlam, of 48, Chaucer Road, Gillingham, whose death on active service was reported in last week's 'News'. He leaves a widow and young daughter, the former being the daughter of Mr and Mrs Jack Yeoman, late of the Westcourt Arms, Gillingham. Six of the deceased's fellow airmen bore the flag-draped coffin and bugler sounded the Last Post and Reveille.

For many years since, pieces of the dark green Armstrong Whitworth Whitley, bearing the Squadron code markings 'GE-O', flown by Brown and Adlam on its last mission, would be found around the Yorkshire moor. The aircraft itself had been at RAF Linton-on-Ouse only since 3 October 1940, but it would always be remembered because of its brave crew, four of which valiantly lost their lives as they fought for their families at home and for the preservation of their land.

Because of the uncertainty of events surrounding Whitley T4171's destruction and the conflicting reports available, it would be a mere assumption to state the exact reason why four men lost their lives as a result of what happened in the early morning hours of 21 October 1940. Whether it was a combination of flak damage, lack of petrol, disorientation and bad weather over the high ground, or whether it fell to a Ju88 nightfighter (the widely accepted opinion), is yet to be convincingly uncovered.

In 1940, when everything hung in the balance for Britain, the RAF pulled together to fend off a powerful enemy that sought its downfall. When the sun was up, Fighter Command fought constantly against the Luftwaffe to prevent bombs falling on British soil, but by night it was Bomber Command that gave Germany a taste of its own medicine.

Throughout the Battle of Britain bomber crews were actively involved in flying dangerous sorties under the cover of darkness across the Channel. The arduous flights were long and cold for bomber crews, because they were equipped with inadequate clothing that did little or nothing to conserve heat. The aircraft navigation equipment was also insufficient for the task at hand, which was often a cause for crews to become lost or unable to find their primary targets. The bombers were also subject to heavy flak and nightfighters, which made every trip over enemy territory more than unsettling for the crews that flew into darkness night after night to disrupt German industry and invasion barges. These early raids were paid for with great sacrifice, and Sergeant Adlam was one of many who gave their lives in the service of their crew and their country, and for the freedom of their loved ones. As I reflect upon the words inscribed by those most dear to Leonard Adlam, I cannot think of a more fitting tribute to one of these courageous airmen than 'Through trials to the stars'. ●

**Below** Portrait of Sergeant Adlam in flying gear. *(David Pritchard)*

SGT/PILOT
LEONARD F. ADLAM
58 SQN RAF VR

DAV PRITCHARD

## CHAPTER FOUR

# DEATH OF A GUNNERY LEADER

SEAN FEAST

TO SURVIVE AS AN AIR GUNNER IN THE SECOND WORLD WAR REQUIRED LARGE AMOUNTS OF COURAGE, SKILL AND LUCK. AS A SERGEANT REAR GUNNER IN VICKERS WELLINGTONS WHO BEGAN HIS OPERATIONAL CAREER IN DECEMBER 1940, JACK BLAIR RODE HIS LUCK FOR ALMOST FOUR YEARS BEFORE, PERHAPS INEVITABLY, THAT LUCK FINALLY RAN OUT. IT WAS CRUEL FATE TO ROB THE COUNTRY OF SUCH A LOYAL SERVANT – A MAN WHO HAD RISEN FROM THE RANKS TO BECOME AN OFFICER AND RESPECTED GUNNERY LEADER IN THE ELITE PATH FINDER FORCE (PFF), BEING TWICE DECORATED FOR GALLANTRY. BUT, AS ONE OF THE 55,573 BOMBER COMMAND AIRCREW WHO MADE THE SUPREME SACRIFICE, HIS STORY IS PERHAPS TYPICAL OF MANY.

Born John Edward Blair in Bigrigg, a small coastal village on the road from White-haven to Egremont, Jack showed an early aptitude for sport, representing Egremont at cricket and playing a prominent part in helping his team win the West Cumberland Junior League two years in succession. He also played rugby for Egremont and football for Egremont and Kells. With his schooling completed, Jack took a job as a clerk on the LMS Railway, but with war looming he joined the Royal Air Force Volunteer Reserve (RAFVR) and volunteered as an air gunner.

Jack's early training was carried out at No. 9 Bombing & Gunnery School (B&GS) Penrhos, arriving on 23 September 1940 for a three-week course. His first flight was taken in an Armstrong Whitworth Whitley piloted by Flight Sergeant McCullum on the 27th, a two-hour trip in which he fired off 150 rounds. He continued to fly with various captains in equally various aircraft, including Hawker Demons and Fairey Battles, until his training was complete, and he passed his exam with a comfortable 79 per cent. The Chief Instructor (CI) remarked that Jack was 'very sound' and that he 'should do well with experience'. His assessment was to prove accurate in so many ways.

Such was the demand for air gunners at that time that within two weeks of finishing his AB Initio course he had been posted to No. 103 Squadron at RAF Newton. The Squadron, then under the command of Wing Commander Charles Littler, a pre-war regular, had only a few months previously been part of the Advanced Air Striking Force (AASF) that had gallantly but forlornly attempted to halt the German advance through France and the Low Countries. In October 1940 it had finally ditched its outdated Fairey Battles, which were replaced by Vickers Wellington 1Cs – one of the mainstays of the early night assault on Germany.

Jack was allocated to 'B' Flight and flew with the flight commander, Flight Lieutenant Leslie Blome-Jones (another pre-war officer), on a practice bombing trip on 8 November. Further flights followed – the usual mix of air firing practices and cross country trips – until he was deemed ready for operations. He had by now been allocated to a regular crew with a regular skipper – Flight Lieutenant Crawford – and a regular aircraft, Wellington 2770.

On the night of 28/29 December, Bomber Command dispatched fifty-nine Handley Page Hampdens, Wellingtons and Whitleys to bomb port installations. Jack's target was Rotterdam, and an uneventful maiden sortie was completed in a little over three hours. Four further trips were undertaken with Crawford to Gelsenkirchen, Düsseldorf and Wilhemshaven (twice) without incident, although Jack recorded good results over the German port on both occasions, observing fires in the target area and large explosions. The Germans admitted that the first attack (on the night of 15/16 January) caused substantial damage, although Bomber Command's early attempt to sink the *Tirpitz* (on 28 February) – which at the time was

**Below** Jack as a
Gunnery Leader
wearing the ribbon
of the Distinguished
Flying Medal and the
Path Finder 'eagle'
clearly visible.
*(Mike King)*

lurking in Wilhelmshaven harbour – proved un-successful. Indeed the 'beast', as it would later be known, avoided many more determined attacks before finally being sunk in November 1944.

Jack settled into a pattern of operations, averaging two or three trips a month. He had the privilege of flying with his flight commander to Kiel 24 April, experiencing an intense barrage of flak and searchlights but still making it home in one piece, only to attack the same target again a week later and discover 10/10ths cloud over the target.

It was customary at that time to partner the novice pilots, or even senior officers with little or no operational experience, with squadron pilots who already had a number of successful trips under their belts. So it was that on 3 May the crew included both Blome-Jones (now a squadron leader) and a Pilot Officer Percival on a sortie to Cologne

that was again hampered by thick cloud. Blome-Jones made for a secondary target in Rotterdam, only to find the target similarly obscured. Not wanting to come home empty handed, they eventually attacked an enemy aerodrome on the coast.

A few nights later, Blome-Jones, with Jack in the rear turret, was accompanied by Wing Commander Brian Lowe. Lowe had taken over command of the Squadron from Charles Littler in April (Lowe was later killed as a Group Captain). It was a small raid comprising only 15 Wellingtons to Saint-Nazaire. Visibility was perfect, and Jack was clearly delighted to note that the photograph taken as their bombs fell recorded a direct hit on the target.

Squadron losses in those first five months of 1941 had been comparatively light, but they were constantly reminded of the dangers of being hit over the target, and the possibility of a long and arduous flight home over the freezing North Sea that would claim so many lives, as crew members went missing without trace. For two days on 16 and 17 May the Squadron sent out various crews to search for missing comrades, to no avail. (Pilot Officer Raymond Eccles RNZAF and crew went missing on the night of 15/16, although four would later survive as prisoners of war.)

A new OC 'B' Flight, Squadron Leader Gordon Lane, replaced Blome-Jones in May (Blome-Jones ended the war as OC No. 630 Squadron) and was Jack's skipper until the end of his tour. The pace of operations increased considerably as spring gave way to summer, with targets primarily clustered around industrial targets, though these sorties were interspersed with raids on major ports and harbour installations, targeting U-boats and Capital ships. Jack continued to annotate points of interest from each raid: Osnabrück (12 June) – very large fire in target area; Brest (13 June) – searchlights and flak very intense; Duisberg (16 June) – searchlights very intense; Kiel (20 June) – 10/10ths over target; Düsseldorf (30 June) – bombs seen bursting on target.

Casualties began to mount. In June the Squadron lost the crews of Flying Officer Robert Chisholm and Squadron Leader Dermot Kelly. Two further crews were lost in July, with the casualties including Sergeant John Bucknole and Sergeant Mervyn Lund. Indeed, July was a month

**Left** No. 103 Squadron Wellington bomber. *(Mike King)*

full of incident. On the 11th, the whole Squadron moved from RAF Newton to its new base at RAF Elsham Wolds in Lincolnshire and two weeks later Jack was involved in a daylight operation to Brest to bomb the Battle Cruisers *Scharnhorst* and *Prinz Eugen*. It was very nearly his last operation.

For three days the Squadron practised formation flying in preparation for the raid that would involve 100 aircraft attacking to a clearly defined plan: three Boeing B-17 Flying Fortresses would attack at 30,000 feet to attract the German fighter defences prematurely; 18 Hampdens escorted by three

squadrons of Supermarine Spitfires would further divert the attentions of the Luftwaffe away from the main force of 79 Wellingtons, which would rely on their own gunners to keep residual fighters at bay. As usual, not everything went strictly according to plan. On the day in question, Jack was rear gunner in Wellington 1588 R-Robert with Squadron Leader Lane and Wing Commander Lowe as pilot and second pilot respectively. They were the lead aircraft in a section of three when their aircraft was attacked by a Messerschmitt Bf109. The combined efforts of all three gunners in the

**Left** Crew of R1588, 103 Squadron, August 1941. Sergeant Blair, Flight Sergeant Wilkinson, Sergeant John Grassom (KIA August 1941), Sergeant Arthur Figg RCAF (KIA August 1941), Pilot Officer Ian Murchie (KIA September 1941), Squadron Leader Lane DFC. *(Mike King)*

**Right** Blair, Figg, Lane, Murchie, Wilkinson and Grassom with members of the ground crew. *(Mike King)*

formation led to the destruction of the enemy, and Jack and his colleagues fought off no fewer than twenty separate attacks by fighters over the target.

This was Jack's first engagement in actual combat, a fact highlighted in the citation for his Distinguished Flying Medal that paid tribute to his professionalism and expertise since joining the Squadron:

This NCO [wrote his Squadron Commander] has at all times shown the highest possible courage and devotion to duty, and has succeeded in achieving an operational record of which the Squadron can be proud.

Sergeant Blair's captain, Squadron Leader Lane, gives him an excellent report and I personally consider his work, both in the air and on the ground, merits the award for which he is recommended. His quiet manner and determined spirit are a valuable asset in the air and have earned the complete confidence of the remainder of the crew, and the Squadron as a whole.

When news of his award was made public (it was published in the *London Gazette* on 21 October 1941), Jack became something of a celebrity in his home town, his local newspaper proclaiming 'DFM for Egremont man'. He was similarly excited enough to send his wife Selina a telegram on the 28th with the simple words 'Got the DFM'.

By this time, Jack had long since completed his first tour, clocking up a total of twenty-seven trips. He was then screened – the process whereby aircrew were taken off operations and diverted into supposedly less 'risky' pastimes, primarily training, where in fact the risk of death at the hands of a novice pilot was still very real indeed. Jack was posted to No. 27 Operational Training Unit (OTU), RAF Lichfield, as a gunnery instructor. He stayed at RAF Lichfield for three months, moving on to No.1 AAS RAF Manby in November 1941, where he qualified as an air gunner instructor on 19 December. Six months later, Jack arrived at the Central Gunnery School (CGS) at RAF Sutton

Bridge to take the Gunnery Leader's course, successfully qualifying with effect from 8 July 1942. On the 31st, while at RAF Tatenhill (part of No. 27 OTU), he sneaked in an operation to Düsseldorf, his first for almost a year, as a guest of Flight Sergeant Chidgey, and two further trips in September with Warrant Officer Tye.

Jack was mentioned in a dispatch in January 1943 'for distinguished service', and his skill as an instructor was clearly much in demand. Indeed, it was not until April 1943 that he was able to return to operations, being obliged first to attend No. 1645 Conversion Unit at RAF Wigsley. The aircraft available to Bomber Command had advanced considerably from the Whitleys, Wellingtons and

Hampdens that had been at the vanguard from the outset of war. Now the four-engined 'heavies' were equipping front-line squadrons, and Jack was crewed with Flight Lieutenant Joseph Sauvage DFC (Sauvage came from the Seychelles) to convert from the twin-engine Manchester onto Avro's more reliable Merlin-powered four-engine Lancaster. Two weeks at RAF Wigsley were followed swiftly by a posting to No. 97 Squadron stationed at RAF Bourn.

The Squadron had only recently arrived at its new base. Previously part of No. 5 Group, No. 97 had been allocated to No. 8 Group (PFF) in April 1943, and was now one of the principal heavy bomber squadrons providing target marking for

**Left** Blair in his office. *(Mike King)*

**Right** EE176 OF-N (Nuts) at Bourn in 1943 – a very special Lanc. She survived 120 operations. *(Mike King)*

Main Force aircraft that followed behind. Jack was back in his element; he was also now Pilot Officer Blair, DFM, a commissioned officer and a gentleman. The Sauvage crew joined the newly formed 'C' Flight, and commenced operations on 4 May, attacking the primary target, Dortmund. Further operations in May included: the long haul to Pilsen on the 13th; Dortmund again on the 23rd; Düsseldorf on the 25th (with the Squadron Commander, Wing Commander Graham Jones DSO, DFC); and Wuppertal in the Ruhr on the 29th. This was midway through the period known as 'The Battle of the Ruhr', at the heart of what the Commander-in-Chief (Harris) called 'his main offensive'. The pace was relentless, the Sauvage crew moving on through the Pathfinder ranks from 'supporter' to 'marker'.

Jack's logbook records a flight to RAF Scampton on 16 June 'on detachment' in preparation for operations on the 20th. His was one of four No. 97 Squadron crews from No. 8 Group supporting a No. 5 Group initiative to trial new marking tech-

niques (there was tremendous rivalry between the two Groups and their Commanders, Donald Bennett and the Honourable Sir Ralph Cochrane). Despite an excellent piece of work by the Sauvage crew, which managed to place a Target Indicator (TI) on the centre of the target (the Zeppelin works at Friedrichshaven), the attack achieved only modest success in terms of damage inflicted. The surprise tactic of the bomber stream flying onwards to Maison Blanche in North Africa, however, completely outfoxed the German nightfighters awaiting their return. Jack eventually returned to RAF Scampton as a passenger of another No. 97 Squadron crew via Gibraltar on the 27th, his aircraft having been damaged by flak.

The Battle of the Ruhr gave way to the Battle of Hamburg at the end of July 1943, Jack taking part in the major raid on the night of 24/25 in which Window – an aluminium strip that disrupted German radar – was used for the first time. The Battle of Hamburg was in turn superseded eventually by the opening round of the Battle of Berlin, the

Sauvage crew making three trips to 'The Big City', on all three occasions in the role of 'Blind Markers', using H2S radar sets to display an image of the target on a cathode ray screen. Sandwiched in between was yet another 'special' raid to the rocket research establishment at Peenemünde on the Baltic. This was the first occasion that a 'Master Bomber' (Group Captain John Searby of No. 83 Squadron) was employed to control a full-scale raid, and it was an outstanding success. All sixteen of the No. 97 Squadron aircraft that marked and bombed the target returned safely.

Jack flew his fifty-seventh operation, and what was to prove his final one with the Squadron, on 6 October as a Blind Marker. Some sixty aircraft executed a diversionary raid on Ludwigshaven to draw enemy fighters away from the main effort to Frankfurt. Soon after he was permanently awarded his Path Finder Force Badge – the celebrated 'eagle' that had been the idea of 'Butch' Harris himself.

It had been a hectic period of operations against some of the Fatherland's most heavily defended

targets, punctuated by the occasional attacks on the Italian cities of Turin and Milan – flights of more than nine hours in duration. The skill of his pilot had been recognized with a Distinguished Service Order (DSO) to add to the DFC he had won in 1942 with No. 44 (Rhodesia) Squadron. Jack's bravery was itself recognized with his own DFC, the citation making mention of the large number of operational sorties completed. It also cited one incident in particular when their aircraft had been attacked by an enemy fighter over Munich:

**Left** Flight Lieutenant (later Squadron Leader) Johnnie Sauvage and his crew standing alongside their Lancaster EE176. (From left) Flight Sergeant Geoff Wood (rear gunner), Flight Sergeant Edwin Wheeler (wireless operator), Sergeant Bill Waller (flight engineer), Flight Lieutenant Johnnie Sauvage (pilot), Flying Officer Jack Blair (mid-upper gunner), Flight Lieutenant Harold Hitchcock (navigator), Flying Officer Peter Burbridge (bomb aimer). *(Kevin Bending)*

Flight Lieutenant Blair's excellent directions to his Captain enabled the attacker to be frustrated. … An excellent air gunner, he has always displayed the greatest keenness to fly on operations and contributed largely to the high standard of gunnery in the unit.

These high standards were much in demand. Posted at the end of November to the Pathfinder Navigation Training Unit (NTU) at RAF Upwood, he spent three months instructing before again returning to operations, this time with No. 156 Squadron PFF.

Bomber Command was now fully employed in its all-out assault on the German capital and its people. In the four months from November 1943 to the end of March 1944, bomber crews carried out no fewer than thirty-two major raids, including sixteen to Berlin. Losses were mounting, and the German nightfighter force was in the ascendancy. On the night of 20/21 February, the No. 156 Squadron Gunnery Leader, acting Squadron Leader Andrew Muir, DFC, failed to return from an operation to Stuttgart; two days later, Jack arrived at No. 156 as his replacement.

It was to Stuttgart, coincidentally, that Jack flew his first trip with the Squadron. Experienced

'Leaders' tended to be crewed with senior flight or squadron commanders, and it was with the 'A' Flight Commander, Squadron Leader Walter Brooks (later Wing Commander, DSO, AFC, OC No. 635 Squadron), that he completed his first operation in almost five months. But it was also not untypical of 'Leaders' to fly with less experienced crews, either so that they could assess their abilities and instil confidence in a comparatively new 'team', or just because there was a spare seat available. Nuremberg was the target for the night of 30 March in a raid that has gone down in history for all the wrong reasons. Of an attacking force of 795 aircraft, 95 were lost – the biggest Bomber Command loss of the war. Four of those aircraft were from No. 156, all the victims of nightfighters. The main raid was also a failure.

After the mauling, there was a brief respite and yet another change in targets, as Bomber Command prepared to play its part in the invasion of Europe. There was still time for some old favourites, however, including an outstandingly successful raid on Friedrichshaven, later described in an American report as 'the most damaging raid on tank production of the war'. Jack flew with Pilot Officer Langford. But success came at a price. Wing Commander Guy Lockhart, DSO, DFC & Bar, OC No. 7 Squadron PFF was shot down and

**Right**
The original cross on the grave of Squadron Leader Blair at Molenaarsgraaf Protestant churchyard. *(Mike King)*

**Far right** Jack Blair's memory is perpetuated on his parents' gravestone in Egremont. *(Mike King)*

**Left** The medals of Squadron Leader Blair, DFC, DFM. *(Mike King)*

killed; closer to home, the No. 156 Squadron Commanding Officer Group Captain Eric Eaton, DFC, was also lost. Such were the fortunes of war that experience was by no means a guarantee of survival.

The invasion was now only a few weeks away. The French port of Boulogne features in Jack's logbook as the target for 19 May (with Squadron Leader Herbert Slade, DFC, RAAF), a simple trip in which they were there and back inside two hours.

Two days after the Boulogne attack, the target was Duisberg. Jack had already been there twice before, and on this occasion his pilot was a young Flight Sergeant called William Ward. The rest of the crew comprised: the flight engineer, Sergeant Sidney Smith; Flight Sergeant Evan Roberts, navigator; Flight Sergeant Raymond Keating, air bomber; Flight Sergeant Raymond Watts, wireless operator; and Sergeant Thomas McCaffery manning the mid-upper turret. Take-off was 2244 hours. At 0100 hours their Lancaster (ND559) was heard circling the village of Molenaarsgraaf (Zuid-Holland). Then the night sky was lit up by a huge explosion, and parts of the burning aircraft began falling all around. They had been stalked and shot down by a German nightfighter piloted by one of the Luftwaffe's 'experts', Hauptmann Martin Drewes. It was his 41st victory. At daybreak, six bodies were found, one in a meadow, others in gardens, and one some way distant. All were carried to the local church.

Soon after, the German commander for the local district (the Orstkommandant) arrived with several soldiers to inspect the bodies that had by

now been laid out, side by side. One of the villagers, in a letter to Selina Blair (Jack's widow) some years later, described them as having peaceful faces, as though they were asleep. Three of the airmen were immediately identified by their dog tags: Blair, Keating, and Smith. Two were identifiable only by their ranks. One remained unknown. One was still missing.

Miraculously, the pilot, William Ward, was still alive. He had been blown clear by the blast and saved on account of wearing a seat-type parachute rather than the clip-on variety issued to the rest of the crew. He confirmed under questioning that the others had stowed their parachutes at the back of the aircraft, and as such had no time to retrieve them when the nightfighter struck. The attack had been too sudden and its outcome too catastrophic.

The personal effects of the dead were gathered and taken by the Germans, and, as the Orstkommandant left, he gave orders that the airmen should be buried immediately, without coffins, in an unmarked grave. The villagers appealed to the remaining German soldiers, who eventually relented. They had two hours in which to make the coffins and bury the dead. Skilled carpenters set to work, and all six coffins were completed in time. At one o'clock that afternoon, the burial took place, with nearly everyone from the local area lining the streets to pay their respects as the procession made its way to the church. They were buried with full military honours.

During the following night, a wooden cross was made and secured to the grave. A jug of beautiful flowers lay alongside. Squadron Leader Jack Blair, DFC, DFM, 32, was at last resting in peace. ●

## CHAPTER FIVE

# LUCK AND SURVIVAL

## STEVE DARLOW

JOHN BANFIELD CONSIDERS HIMSELF EXTREMELY FORTUNATE TO HAVE SURVIVED HIS TIME WITH BOMBER COMMAND. MANY VETERAN AIRCREW PUT THEIR SURVIVAL DOWN TO SIMPLE GOOD FORTUNE. 'I WAS VERY LUCKY' IS ONE OF THE MOST COMMON STATEMENTS MADE BY VETERANS OF THE RAF'S BOMBING CAMPAIGN WHEN QUESTIONED ON HOW THEY GOT THROUGH IT. JOHN BANFIELD IS CERTAINLY ONE OF THOSE WHO CONSIDERS HIMSELF LUCKY TO HAVE SURVIVED. DEATH HAD STALKED JOHN, BUT GOOD FORTUNE AND QUIRKS OF FATE KEPT HIM ALIVE – SO JOHN COULD TELL HIS TALE.

**Left** RAF Blackpool, September 1940, wireless operator training. John Banfield is second row up, second from left. *(John Banfield)*

Born in harrow, Middlesex, on 15 May 1920, John Banfield grew up in south London and became captivated by the sounds and sights of Croydon and Biggin Hill aerodromes as he gazed wondrously from their perimeters. When John first went to volunteer for aircrew duties, he was denied, owing to the fact that he replied 'No' when asked by the recruiting officer if he had permission to join. John returned a couple of days later, was asked exactly the same questions and gave the same reply. 'The chap said "What's your name?" I was in.' Sworn in at Uxbridge in June 1940 and following some 'square bashing', John was sent to Blackpool and started on the Morse code table, training for wireless operator duties. Over the next few months John's postings took him around the country, raising his Morse words-per-minute and literally getting to grips with gunnery training. Finally he ended up at No. 14 Operational Training Unit at RAF Cottesmore on Handley Page Hampdens and Avro Ansons. Quickly the harsh realities of war became all too apparent. Training for aircrew duties had its own inherent dangers. New recruits and novices had to test their skills in wartime conditions and not necessarily on the best aircraft. Accidents were numerous – over 8,000 aircrew were killed while training:

There were 3 occasions when I was detailed as a pallbearer – the accidents at Cottesmore. The previous course got practically wiped out. On one occasion we knew that for one chap there were very few remains. The 6 of us, with 3 either side of the coffin, went to lift it up imagining the weight of a man. It flew up in the air. I saw some horrible things, chaps losing their lives. Even on the squadron a few times I volunteered to attend funerals.

Despite having to cope with such experiences, John does not recall it adversely affecting his morale at the time. 'Remarkable when I think back. It didn't worry me that I might get shot up.' Yet during the interview for this article, seventy years after the event, it is clear that such experiences still do affect John emotionally.

John was posted to an operational unit, No. 207 Squadron, in September 1941, at RAF Waddington, arriving as a 'spare bod'. Before he could join a crew, severe stomach pains meant a visit to sick quarters, a diagnosis of Paratyphoid fever, and five weeks in hospital. Despite a full recovery, John thought it was the end of his flying days, but the No. 1 Central Medical Board RAF Halton granted him permission to return to his Squadron. He was

We went in at about 15,000 feet and bombed. Then I looked down and saw 2 headlights moving out. I said, 'Dim, what are those two lights there?' He said, 'I don't know, we'll go down and have a look.' It was a train and he got me to shoot it up with the two front guns. All of a sudden it disappeared – apparently the blasted train went through a tunnel. We came out at low level. I don't suppose it was much, about 500 feet, and there were all these searchlights. I was lining up the one in front of me ready to shoot it up, but the bugger went out before I got there.

John's next raid, again in a Manchester, was to Brest on 25 January 1942, when he was again flying as a spare bod with a Flying Officer 'P. O. Prune' Leland, in the front gun turret. It was three months before John was next operational, as crews completed their conversions to the four-engine Avro Lancaster bombers.

In November 1940, 207 Squadron was reformed, with the then new Manchester bomber, which was plagued with many problems, especially with the Rolls Royce Vulture engines. With a great sigh of relief, in March 1942, we became the third squadron to complete conversion to the four-engine Lancaster bomber.

In March 1942 John was crewed up with Sergeant John McCarthy. The third operation penned into John Banfield's logbook records a 'Nickel' (that is, a leaflet raid) to Marseilles on 3 May 1942. Then, on 29 May, the McCarthy crew was detailed for a mining operation in the Sound of Copenhagen.

As we were going out over Denmark the searchlight came on and the ack-ack started. I lowered the guns down and fired straight into them and they went out. The pilot managed to swerve and got out of the line of fire. If he hadn't have done so we would have been shot out of the sky. He levelled off and they opened up again. One shell burst in the tail elevator and a piece of shrapnel went through the rear gunner's arm. He survived and subsequently spent some time in hospital, but the poor chap eventually joined another crew and got killed in action. (*The wounded gunner was a*

**Above** John Banfield in flying gear, 1942. (*John Banfield*)

keen to put all his training into practice, but bureaucracy was John's immediate enemy. When he arrived back at Waddington, he discovered the Squadron had been posted to RAF Bottesford. With time to kill in the two months for a transfer to come through, he 'got to know Lincoln Cathedral inside out'. Just before Christmas the posting to the Squadron arrived, but as there was no prospect of being crewed up he was sent on leave.

In January 1942, John, in his capacity as a wireless operator/air gunner, remained a spare bod replacing sick aircrew. He started to gain experience on the twin-engine Avro Manchester, replacing the sick front gunner in Flying Officer 'Dim' Wooldridge's crew (which included a second pilot, Sergeant John McCarthy) on a raid to Münster on 22 January 1942.

*Sergeant Arthur Roddam. On the night of 16/17 August 1942, Sergeant Roddam held rear gunner responsibilities on No. 207 Squadron's Lancaster R5509 EM-N, which was lost without trace on a minelaying operation. The entire crew of seven is commemorated on the Air Forces Memorial at Runnymede.)*

The very next day, following their eventful mine-laying trip, John's crew found themselves detailed to take part in one of the most momentous and significant bombing operations of the entire war, the 30/31 May 1942 'Thousand Bomber Raid' to Cologne. RAF Bomber Command's Commander-in-Chief, Air Chief Marshal Sir Arthur Harris, was making a significant statement of his command's destructive capability, calling upon training commands ultimately to send 1,047 bomb-laden aircraft to the German city of Cologne.

We were due to bomb in the last 20 minutes of the raid, but before we crossed the Dutch coast we could see Cologne on fire. When we got there

there was very little opposition so we bombed quite easily. I will always remember, being in the nose, then all of a sudden I saw a chute come down and the skipper pulled the aircraft up and over him. That was over Cologne which was a mass of flame – really shocking. They'd bombed London and also Coventry. We didn't give a damn about the loss of life. We were determined to give them their own medicine. They'd 'reap the whirlwind' as Bomber Harris said.

John's logbook continued to fill with operational details. His sixth operation was to Essen on 1 June, then Essen again on 16 June and Emden on 20 June. Another attack on Emden on 22 June was followed by two attacks on Bremen on 25 and 29 June, against the latter of which John wrote in his logbook: 'a/c shot up'. John recalls: 'We were caught in a heavy ack-ack box barrage, which resulted in shrapnel damage to the fuselage.' Two minelaying trips on 3 and 12 July preceded an operation to Vegesack's U-boat yards on 19 July.

**Left** John Banfield's logbook, showing the entries for May 1942, including the Thousand Bomber Raid on Cologne. *(John Banfield)*

With fourteen operations now completed, John was offered the opportunity to retrain. With the dangers of training still fresh in John's mind, he was initially reluctant.

Halfway through ops they asked me if I would like to remuster as a bomb aimer. I said 'Go to hell. I'm not going back to Training Command.' 'No. No. No,' they said. 'You'll do the training on

**Right**
John Banfield's first pilot, John McCarthy, peering out of a Lancaster, around June 1942.
*(John Banfield)*

the squadron.' 'Oh.' I replied, 'OK Count me in.' If I hadn't said that I wouldn't be talking now. I had to come off my crew and 3 days later the crew went down – every man was killed in action. The fact that I remustered saved my life. *(No. 207 Squadron Lancaster R5867 EM-T was lost on 23/24 July 1942 raid to Duisberg. The aircraft fell to earth near Krefeld, where the crew were initially buried. All are now interred at the Reichswald Forest War Cemetery).*

| |
|---|
| *Pilot Officer J. J. N. McCarthy RNZAF* |
| *Flight Sergeant J. D. L. La Salle RCAF* |
| *Flight Sergeant E. A. Edmonds* |
| *Flight Sergeant J. M. Leahy* |
| *Flight Sergeant A. Rowland* |
| *Sergeant D. Worthington* |
| *Pilot Officer E. L. Hayward* |

As a bomb aimer, in September 1942, John joined his new crew, skippered by a Sergeant Chaster. John's tally of operations steadily built: minelaying

(9 September), Wismar (23 September), mine-laying (24 September), Aachen (5 October), Osnabrück (6 October), Le Creusot (17 October), Genoa (22 October), Milan (24 October), mine-laying (27 October) and Turin (28 November). Then on 3 January 1943 the then Flight Sergeant Chaster took his crew on an operation testing the relatively new electronic blind bombing technique named Oboe – take-off 1715 hours in Lancaster W4134 EM-U. Against this aircraft 'Failed to Return' was later added to the Squadron records. John recalls, 'It was an experimental raid – blind bombing. All I had to do was aim at a white flare that was laid by Pathfinders using Oboe. We actually overshot the first flare, by less than a minute. I heard the rear gunner pipe up, 'John, the flare's gone off.'' Despite the dangers Chaster brought the aircraft round again, John stating he would 'catch the red' flare.

Which I did. The weather forecaster had said 8/10ths cloud over the target. When we got there it was 2/10ths and the bloody searchlights came through. We could see the master searchlight winding round until it hit us and then about 20 others came in. We were coned several times.

Chaster managed to escape the searchlights and bring his crew and aircraft clear of the immediate danger. Then, as the Lancaster roared westwards,

crossing the Dutch–German border between Roermond and Venlo, a stalking German night-fighter pilot, vectored by German ground control, seized his chance.

I was back up in the turret, we were weaving a bit, and all of a sudden I saw tracer come up. I lifted up my feet and thought 'Oh my God!' The first shot went straight through the centre of gravity of the aircraft, straight through the batteries, and the intercom went. I lowered my guns to try and get at the fighter, but I couldn't see him. All I could

see was tracer. With us weaving the rest of the shots went into the starboard side and set the petrol alight behind the inboard motor. I felt someone pulling on my trouser leg so I got out. It was the navigator, 'We've got to bale out.'

I put my chute on and went to the hatch in the nose – couldn't move it. I reckon the cannon shell had caught it. Normally speaking you could either push it out or pull it in. I said to the nav get out through the back door. I looked back to the main spar, and there was a petrol line flaring away. 'Oh my God.' I followed the nav up and saw him disappear out of the side of the aircraft where the Perspex blister had been shattered by cannon shell. 'Bloody Hell,' I thought, 'the inboard motor propeller is within a foot of that.' I looked out and could see that the flight engineer, who was OK when I got out, had feathered the inboard motor. The petrol behind it was on fire. I saw the navigator get clear so I followed suit. We were going near on 200 m.p.h. and the slipstream caught me. I was swept round. My chute, which was still attached, was inside the aircraft and I was outside. I reached my arm back inside to get my chute, hugged it to my chest and went under the mainplane, striking the tail unit with my shoulder.

**Left** John Banfield on the wing of a Lancaster, June 1942, RAF Bottesford. (*John Banfield*)

**Left** John Banfield, Lancaster wireless operator, June 1942. (*John Banfield*)

No. 207 Squadron
Lancaster at RAF
Bottesford, 1942.
*(John Banfield)*

John passed out and recalls nothing of his descent. When he came to he was swinging like a pendulum. 'My chute was caught in a great tall tree.'

It was snowing like mad. I couldn't release myself from the harness – I had another 20 feet to go. All I could do was call out. It must have been 20 minutes, perhaps more, when I saw a row of torches coming towards me. I think they were crop watchers and there were a couple of German airmen with them. One saw my predicament, went away, and came back with a ladder. He put crampons on, climbed up, transferred me from my chute to a rope, and lowered me down. I couldn't stand up, so they lashed me to the ladder, using it as a stretcher, and took me to a farmhouse. There was a big kitchen with a big

table and they laid me out. The family were all there and the grandmother tended my face which was cut and bleeding. I was a bit of a mess. My shoulder was paining like mad. Suddenly a German officer came in, I think an SS man, and he bawled at the rest of the family to get out, but allowed the granny to carry on tending me. He came over and said 'Sprechen Sie Deutsch? 'No,' I replied. With that he went out and shortly after 2 German airmen came in, helped me out, and took me to the sick quarters at Venlo airfield. It was about 1 o'clock at night.

The Medical Officer was awoken. John was given an anaesthetic, told he had not broken any bones,

and then taken to a cell. 'There were blankets on the floor and one of the guards who could speak English said, "Would you like some more blankets." I said, "No, No." All I wanted to do was go to sleep. I was whacked.' The following morning, after a restless night, then a cup of ersatz coffee for breakfast, John was carried by German guards to a car, and driven to a rail station. 'On the platform I saw another chap on a stretcher. A voice piped up, "Is that you John?" It was my navigator.' Both men were hospitalized in Amsterdam. 'A quarter of it had been taken over by the Luftwaffe. Quite honestly I wouldn't have been medically treated better had the same thing happened in England. It would have been a different tale if we had been caught by the Army. I was fortunate to be in the hands of the Luftwaffe.' *(John, his pilot and his navigator, Sergeant Marwood, survived the incident. The four other members of the crew, Sergeant Moger, Sergeant Pugh, Sergeant Lineker, and Sergeant Harris, were killed and initially buried at Venlo – their bodies subsequently taken to Jonkerbos War Cemetery. Flight Sergeant Chaster managed to evade capture, be taken into an evasion line and transported through France to the Pyrenees, crossing the Spanish border and ending up in Gibraltar. Chaster returned to the UK by boat and was prevented from going back on operations, in case he should be caught again and thereby compromise the secrecy surrounding the evasion line.)*

Following a day's rest, aided with a sleeping powder, John was taken to a room with a barred window and six beds, some already occupied: an Australian with a lot of shrapnel in his back, a heavily bandaged Pole 'in a pretty poor state', another airman with a shattered tibia and fibia, and another badly burnt man who had been on Special Operations Executive duties and dragged from a burning Halifax bomber by a German officer – 'eventually he was repatriated'. After four weeks, John, his navigator, the Australian and the airman with the broken leg were sent to the German Air Force Prisoner of War transit camp, DulagLuft. John was put in isolation.

**Left** Prisoner of war John Banfield at Lamsdorf, bottom right, 9 October 1943. *(John Banfield)*

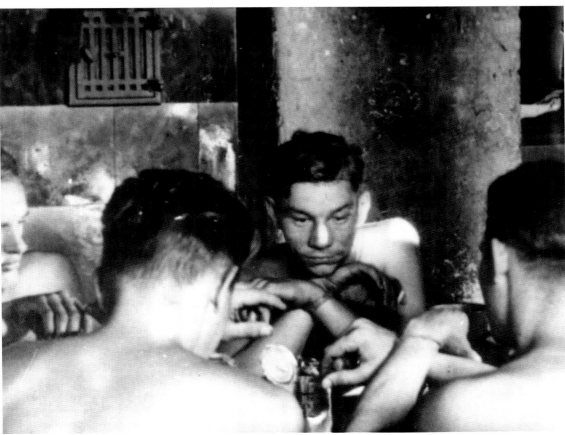

**Left** Lamsdorf POWs tied up with string, 1942. *(John Banfield's collection)*

**Right** Lamsdorf. A POW shows off his manacles, 1942-43. *(John Banfield's collection)*

We had been briefed what to expect and it turned out exactly that. I was still feeling rough. They put the heat up, that was one of the tricks. An interrogation officer came in. He bawled at me, 'Don't you stand when an officer comes in?' I responded, 'I'm not familiar with the German uniforms yet.' He said, 'Were you wounded?' I said, 'Yes', and he replied, 'Oh I'm sorry.' He started soft-soaping me. I knew what he was up to. I got up, sat at a table and there was a portfolio of 207 Squadron.

John did his best not to express any signs of re-cognition. 'He turned the sheets over and I looked towards the end of a list. I saw the names of my old crew. Each man had a cross against his name. It wasn't until then that I knew how close I had been to being killed in action. I tried to stave off any emotion.' John, on being presented with a 'Red Cross' questionnaire, recalled warnings of such false documents and gave only his name, rank and

number. His interrogator persisted, 'Don't be bloody stupid we know everything.' 'Well you bloody well put it down because I am not going to,' John responded. His interrogator then displayed an ability to express himself with English expletives and promised to return later. After a couple of days the questionnaire ruse was repeated. 'They said, "Oh it will help the office." I replied, "I'm not interested in helping your bloody office."' Finally John was left alone and shortly after was transferred to StalagLuft VIIIB at Lamsdorf, Poland, arriving in February 1943, initially chained up as part of the continuing reprisal for the shackling of German prisoners following the Allied Dieppe raid in August 1942. John recalls that this went on until September 1943, at which point he, along with fellow POWs, were allowed out of the compound to walk around the rest of the camp.

John's incarceration continued through to January 1945, when the POWs began to hear guns

**Right** A POW listening in on the illegal crystal set at Lamsdorf, 1943. *(John Banfield)*

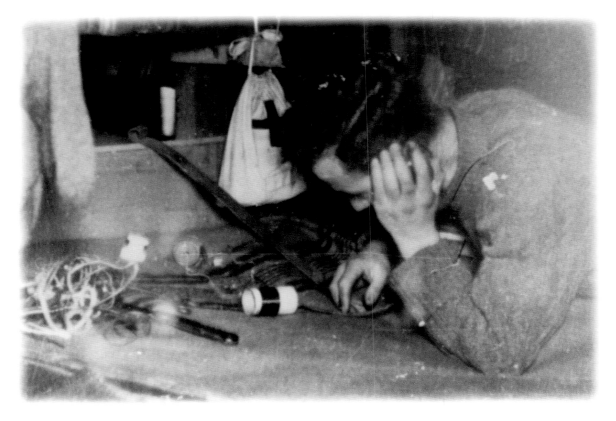

rumbling to the east, manned by the advancing Russian forces. The camp was evacuated and thousands of bedraggled POWS, in columns, began to trek west. John kept falling back, 'I thought blow this for a lark, I'm going to feign sickness. I got away with it and fell out with twenty others, half had frostbite on their feet. The rest of the column went on and left us with one guard.' Housed in a farm, managed by Poles, the POWs were given some dehydrated vegetables and made soup. 'Did that go down well!' Eventually another column from the POW camp at StalagLuft VII, Bankau, arrived; 'they were in a shocking state'. John joined the column and after two short marches they were entrained: 'Sixty men to a cattle truck. We couldn't all sit down at the same time and were like that for two and a half days, and only let out once. Some chaps had foolishly eaten frozen vegetables they had picked up on the road and suffered dysentry.'

Eventually John arrived at StalagLuft IIIA, Luckenwalde, where he remained, suffering food shortage, overcrowding and squalid conditions, until the Russians arrived in April, 'in tanks and literally went straight through our camp, straight through the wire. This was the spearhead and there were women as well. After a couple of days the troops of occupation came in and invited us to do some fighting. We declined.' Delay followed while the Russian, and British, and American 'Allies' discussed the release of their captured servicemen. Eventually the Russians transported the POWs to Wittenberg, where a pontoon bridge crossed the River Elbe. 'It was a case of 50 of us going across and 50 Russian POWs from western Germany, who didn't want to return, forced back at gun point.'

John had played his part in the bomber offensive against Germany. He had survived the dangers of training and operations, thankful not to have been with his first crew when they made their sacrifice, and fortunate, unlike fellow crew mates, to have survived being shot down. Many surviving aircrew, like John, were similarly lucky, and many take the responsibility of remembering those who did not make it through the ordeal – at squadron reunions, association meetings and memorial unveilings. At such events, raw emotions are kept in check, just like they were decades previously; nevertheless they

are still there.

John left the air force shortly after his return to England in 1945, owing to ear problems. Post-war John worked in the printing business. He is currently the secretary and treasurer of the Royal Air Forces Ex-Prisoner of War Association and was awarded the MBE for his services to the association. John is clear on his feelings concerning RAF Bomber Command's contribution to the war, the sacrifice made and the lack of recognition.

I remember after the Thousand Bomber Raid, they read us a signal from the Prime Minister. He was jumping around like a cat on hot bricks. Yet at the end of the war he changed his tune. We were defeating Nazism. If it hadn't been for Bomber Command, the Germans would have been over here. The loss we suffered: nearly half the chaps who volunteered for aircrew duties in the war lost their lives. I was a POW at Lamsdorf, and in the compound there was 1,000 aircrew. Amongst them you could count the number of complete crews on one hand. They were all parts of crews, like mine. ●

**Left** Warrant Officer John Banfield, June/July 1945.
*(John Banfield)*

## CHAPTER SIX

# 'CAN I GIVE YOU A HUG?'

## JULIAN EVAN-HART

TIME IS THE EVER-MARCHING AND UNCONTROLLABLE COMMODITY, THE MEASUREMENT OF ALL MANKIND'S HISTORY, PAST AND PRESENT AS WELL AS FUTURE. THIS IS THE REMARKABLE TIMELINE ACCOUNT OF A SECOND WORLD WAR BOMBER: THE THREE SECONDS IT TOOK TO DESTROY IT, AND THE FIFTY-THREE YEARS IT TOOK TO RECOVER ITS WRECKAGE AND THOSE OF ITS CREW, WHO HAD REMAINED MISSING FOR SO LONG. THERE WERE NUMEROUS ROYAL AIR FORCE AIR CRASHES IN EUROPE DURING THE YEARS 1939–45. ALL WERE TRAGEDIES OF WARFARE, AND MANY WERE SIMILAR IN FACTUAL BACKGROUND TO THE FATE OF THIS PARTICULAR HEAVY BOMBER. HOWEVER, A FEW SUCH INCIDENTS STAND OUT, BECAUSE OF EVENTS THAT TAKE PLACE MANY YEARS AFTERWARDS AND THAT ARE MOSTLY DICTATED AND CREATED BY THE DEDICATED ACTIONS OF AVIATION ARCHAEOLOGICAL GROUPS SUCH AS THE BELGIAN AVIATION HISTORY ASSOCIATION (BAHA). TO THE FAMILIES OF THE AIRCREW LOST ON A DARK MAY NIGHT IN 1944, IT WAS A TRAGEDY OF MONUMENTAL INDESCRIBABLE ANGUISH; TO THEIR FELLOW SQUADRON COLLEAGUES, IT WAS A PAINFUL REMINDER OF THEIR OWN MORTALITY.

To almost everyone else during those hectic years it was just a loss, pretty much the expected norm; to a few it was even further removed from any emotions whatsoever, being simply a statistic. Sadly since the end of the war, the swift progress of time has thinned out eyewitnesses to such events; grieving parents have long since passed away, and even the 65-year-old-plus children of such crews are sometimes resigned to 'My Dad was shot down over Europe somewhere, I don't know much else.' However, things are changing. Grandchildren with their access to the computer age are in many cases attempting, through the fascination of genealogy, to make up for the previous period when details concerning their relatives were largely unavailable. There can be little dispute that, through the efforts of aviation archaeology and its associated research, many of these forgotten bombers and crews are being brought to life again. From piles of twisted oil-soaked and clay-enshrined wreckage, incredible details of long-ago combats and losses can be gleaned, and in some cases those crew members who had been lost to history are finally found, recovered and buried with befitting honours, often providing long-awaited closure to families who never really knew what had happened.

It has been said that 'aviation archaeology has the profound ability to make an aeroplane and its crew "fly again", albeit for perhaps a few hours'. In the case of this epic account, it will be seen that the BAHA not only made this Halifax 'fly again' but also provided an everlasting memorial to this crew and consequently to all Allied aircrews who flew those perilous skies. Aviation archaeology is not simply about souvenir hunting, as some ignorant people may consider. It can have other far more significant implications. In this particular case, the elements of pure dedication, closure for kin, conservation and human forgiveness are all involved. This is a remarkable story, and one that owes much to all involved, particularly Cynrik De Decker and his colleagues in the BAHA. I feel incredibly privileged to be a part of its telling.

An hour or so after take-off from Venlo, Hauptmann Martin Drewes of III Gruppe, Nacht-jagdgeschwader 1 (III/NJG1), his Bordfunker

Oberfeldwebel Erich Handtke and Bordschutze Oberfeldwebel George Petz sat securely, confined in the oil, dope and rubber-smelling cockpit of their Messerschmitt Bf110 G-4, coded G9+MD. The faint whistling shriek from the frontal mounted 'Hirschgeweih' antennae array of their FuG 220 Lichtenstein radar was just audible above the throaty hum of the engines. It was the night of 12/13 May 1944, and they were out once again, as on many previous nights, looking for targets from the streams of RAF bombers that were operational in their zone around Brussels. The skies were crammed with potential targets, and they had already claimed two aircraft, which had been destroyed at 0044 hours and 0049 hours. It was not too long before they made another contact just south of Brussels. This soon became a visual. Here, as always, they had to be careful. Just a quick flash of light from their cockpit or a smooth airframe surface, reflected off a bright moon or perhaps the target fires glowing far below, could give the game away. It was a game in which the dorsal and rear-turret gunners of their intended victims would be straining their eyes to bursting point in order to gain the advantage. However, the aeroplane in front of them had an additional ventral defence, intended

**Below** The pilot of Halifax LW682 Wilbur Boyd Bentz, while training in Canada. *(Unless indicated all images Courtesy of Cynrik De Decker of the Belgian Aviation History Association)*

to combat the nightfighter threat, in the form of a Browning 0.50-calibre gun in a Preston-Green mounting. But if they dropped to an angle behind and below the bomber, that would hopefully give them some security from such prying eyes as well as from the bomber's Monica tail-warning radar.

At 0109 hours Drewes and his crew began slowly to gain on the intended victim. There were surely other enemy bombers in close proximity, but a lack of twinkling streaking tracer indicated that they remained unseen. The Me110 was now being slightly buffeted by the RAF bomber's slipstream, which they clearly identified as a four motor with large twin tail fins – an Avro Lancaster or a Handley Page Halifax. There was still no tracer and best of

armament that would come into play here; it would be the coupled drum-fed 20mm MGFF upward firing cannon nicknamed Schräge Musik. Drewes had again been unconventional, fitting this appliance behind his seat, whereas normally it was further back, adjacent to the Bordfunkers position.

The 'four motor' was now directly above them, presenting a massive target, so Drewes throttled back a small adjustment, which allowed the bomber to slip forward over them for a fraction of a second. They would now aim for the engine inner wing root area of the starboard wing. Thousands of gallons of high octane aviation fuel lay in tanks here, but terrifyingly close by was the fully laden bomb bay, so the aim had to be perfect. Crippling

**Flying Officer Thomas Taylor** (navigator)

**Pilot Officer John Summerhayes** (mid-upper gunner)

**Pilot Officer Joseph Arbour** (mid-under gunner)

**Sergeant Roy Ellerslie** (flight engineer)

all no violent evasive manoeuvres. They continued unseen, lurking in the gloom. With heartbeats pounding in their ears, the members of the nightfighter's three-man crew strained to get a clearer view of the target. Suddenly their view was filled with the massive aeroplane above and slightly off to one side. Its identity was confirmed: it was definitely an Allied four-motored aircraft. The anticipation was immense. Drewes had insisted on being unconventional by retaining the older style frontal armament of two 20mm cannons surmounted by four 7.92mm MG17 machine guns; he considered the later-fitted MK108 30mm cannons caused too much debris to detach from victims, had too low a muzzle velocity and posed far too high a risk in the darkness. However, it was not the forward

the starboard inner engine would, as Drewes well knew, disable the rear turret of either a Lancaster or a Halifax, thus permitting a *coup de grâce* rear attack to dispatch their victim if required. Now their victim became centrally positioned in the upper cockpit gun-sight. For a breath taking split second it was like looking through a large camera lens with unsteady hands. That was it! The Schräge Musik opened up. Wispy fizzling streaks of the feint tracer known as 'Glim Spurr' threaded upwards towards the target. Standard high visibility tracer was not used in the loading sequence. This would have alerted other bomber crews to their presence and also indicated the unusual angle of attack, which RAF High Command in turn would have undoubtedly taken further measures to counteract. Closer, and closer, and closer: Drewes and his crew were no more than 35 metres below the huge aeroplane. Up above, the crew of the four-motored aircraft had absolutely no idea of the imminent danger below. The twin muzzles of the Schräge Musik installation flashed, and there once again was that satisfying repetitive thud in Drewes's back confirming no failure in the compressed air-cocking bottles. Looking upwards the nightfighter crew saw the aim had been true.

The time it took each cannon shell, weighing on average 100 grams, to travel from the end of the Schräge Musik twin barrels to LW682 was just the tiniest part of a single second. The mix of armour-piercing, high-explosive and incendiary rounds impact holes and then detonated immediately, with a blinding white flash and ear-splitting 'crack'. These detonations blew each milled steel cannon shell casing into hundreds of pieces of jagged splinters. Each impacting and exploding shell blew great sections of airframe from the bomber, as rivets were ripped apart and the surrounding airframe pierced by shotgun-effect shrapnel impacts. Delicate wiring and pipe work were smashed away from around the engines in violent sharp explosions. The incendiary rounds had ignited the clouds of fuel vapour released from the punctured fuel tanks. Throttling back further, Drewes allowed the impacts to edge backwards, violently flashing along the under wing, but the nightfighter pilot was care-

**Flying Officer
Clifford Phillips**
(bomb aimer)

**Pilot Officer
Jack McIntyre**
(wireless operator/air
gunner)

**Pilot Officer
Fred Roach**
(rear gunner)

**Pilot Officer
Wilbur Bentz**
(pilot)

ripped into the Halifax's starboard under wing and engine, as desired. A series of violent white flashes illuminated the target area of their victim. While those white explosive flashes signified satisfaction to the Me110 nightfighter crew, they were the cause of panic and terror as they were seen and felt by the bomber crew. The sharper-point-tipped armour-piercing 20mm shells created neat circular impact holes, flaking the black paint for centimetres around them as they punched through the thin airframe. Jagged edges fringed their exit holes, carrying on piercing through lighter construction and pipe work and back out into the darkness or perhaps embedding themselves deeply into engine cylinder pots and perforating the main spar. The blunter nosed high-explosive shells made larger ful to avoid the bomb bay. Suddenly a great streak of orange flame and debris erupted from beneath the bomber and then trailed backwards in a huge banner. Just three seconds had passed since the first cannon shells had sped away towards their target.

Inside the bomber the attack had been a total surprise, and so fast. The bomber's crew had literally no idea what had hit them before their world was turned into sheer chaos. Now confident that no rear attack was necessary, Drewes throttled forward again and quickly manoeuvred his Me110, diving away to port side, denying the opportunistic threat from any doomed but plucky gunners. Neither did he fancy his chances beneath tons of earthbound flaming metal. The increasing glow from the burning Halifax illuminated the numerous victory bars on the twin tailfins of the grey and violet dapple-camouflaged German nightfighter. Someone would be painting on three more in the morning – that was for sure. As they speedily withdrew from the illuminated sky, Drewes and Bordfunker Erich Handtke could clearly see the crippled bomber above them. It maintained level flight for a short time, huge flames trailing in its wake, and then, as if resigned to its fate, it lurched upwards, flipped over and wobbled from side to side, as it started its plunge earthwards. Because of the incredible centrifugal forces, the men inside the burning bomber were trapped with little or no chance of bailing out.

Drewes and his crew later returned to Venlo and landed safely. All they knew about the incident was that yet another victory had been achieved over the RAF Terror Fliegers. They knew nothing of the death and terror caused inside their last 'kill' or indeed any other; no names of those concerned, nothing of their families, the children these men left behind, what squadron they came from. Why should they? There was simply no need; this was war. When achieving an aerial victory, most combatants considered that they were shooting down an aeroplane and preferred to disassociate the action from the fact that the aeroplane also contained fellow human beings. Success was the driving force. Such fine details were of no consequence. In just the same way, enemy bomber crews knew nothing of the casualties they caused. This was indeed total war. Nearly six decades later this 'disassociation' would incredibly be changed for ever for one of the Messerschmitt Bf110's surviving crew, who had been involved in this combat.

Returning to 12/13 May 1944 at 0112 hours, what was the German nightfighter crew's third claim of that night was now spiralling downwards, seemingly in slow motion. A huge sheet of flame engulfed the bomber, giving it the appearance of some earth-bound extraterrestrial comet. The massive teardrop-shaped fireball wavered in its descent, allowing fleeting glimpses of the frontal section and several engine cowlings, the wingtips and just occasionally a tailfin, as the flame momentarily thinned. Plummeting thousands of feet, the bomber,

weakened by the impact of cannon shells and the heat of the fire, began to disintegrate. The slipstream now began to rip away great sections of skinning from the wings. Pieces of flammable material became detached and spiralled into the night sky, each creating a short-lived mini replica of the main flaming mass. Inside the stricken bomber we can but picture the terror of the young crew. Some may already have been injured or even killed by the odd stray cannon shell or ricocheting debris. Trapped in their flaming coffin, they would have descended agonizingly through thousands of feet, tumbling uncontrollably, feeling the intense heat, and perhaps hearing the screams of fellow crew members. For those crew members alive in the latter stages, the final impact would have been a mercy. The giant bomber approached the ground at just over 200 miles an hour. The huge yellow-tipped propeller blades were still rotating under full power as the roaring, flame-bathed mass hit the soft ground of an area of woodland near Schendelbeke close to Geraardsbergen, Belgium.

At an almost vertical angle, the stricken bomber crashed its way through the branches of several trees before impacting on the ground. The Plexiglas nose cone had almost totally melted away by this stage, and the first structure to hit the ground was the frontal fuselage. This instantly compacted, crushing the remains of crew members and contorting into a crumpled mass, as it rammed into the ground. Fractions of a second later the giant propeller blades hit the soft earth, while still rotating, initially ripping up great divots of earth before they were violently twisted backwards and wrapped around each engine. Now a massive yellow and orange fireball exploded, fringed with thick black smoke that seemed to swirl and billow into the night sky. The countryside for miles around was momentarily illuminated, and then night crept back as the flames died down. The huge Bristol Hercules XIV radial engines partially disintegrated, the cylinder pots splitting away as the reduction gears and bosses continued punching through the soft earth, rammed further by the vast weight of the impacting wreckage behind. The wingtips were torn away aft of each outer engine and the now streamlined impacting bulk still continued to split and smash deeper into the waterlogged soil. Within just a couple of seconds, the shattered sections of frontal fuselage and several engines, some now minus their bosses and blades, had punched into the dark soil to a depth of 30 feet. The rear fuselage and tail section were literally concertinaed by the tremendous forces exerted upon them and buckled, with the panels bursting and ripping apart, scattering mangled rivet heads over the surrounding damp woodland floor. The mid-upper turret momentarily burst out of its mounting before being crushed and pulled deep into the ground. The rear fuselage and tail sections collapsed and were smashed into the crater.

Three important critical seconds had passed that night, and eight young men had just lost their lives. The main wreckage containing their bodies now lay in a deep crater of churned oily mud, shattered tree branches, crumpled wreckage, wires, exploding ammunition and some large areas of fire. Several sections of crumpled wingtip lay adjacent to the main crater; smoke drifted in the slight breeze, filling the woodland, as molten aluminium alloy droplets fizzed and sizzled in the freshly disturbed soil. After some ten minutes the smoke and flames lessened, but the sounds of creaking wreckage and crackling small fires were punctuated occasionally by an exploding 0.303 bullet and the cry of several startled tawny owls from among the dark trees.

The next day the German recovery crew managed to locate the remains of five airmen; the bodies of three aircrew were not located and officially were classed as missing. The official German report indicates recovery was incredibly difficult, given the soft marshy terrain near the Dender River. The five bodies located were later buried at the Geraardsbergen Communal Cemetery. It was almost certain that other human remains were present here. Unable to be located, they were thus condemned to remain among the tangled wreckage of their bomber for ever – or were they?

So just what type of aircraft had Martin Drewes's crew been responsible for shooting down at 0109 hours as their third victory of the night, in those dark wartime skies so long ago? Despite the fact that the airbase their victim had flown from would have been aware of its loss, quite where it had crashed was probably unknown, and associated details of the incident would have been scant for years to come. However, modern-day research can confirm that this was indeed a Halifax Mk III and it had the serial number of LW682. This particular aircraft had been delivered by the English Electric Company between 29 February and 3 March 1944. Records also show that it had previously been damaged during a training flight, repaired and then passed on to the Royal Canadian Air Force for operational use with No. 426 (Thunderbird) Squadron, where it was coded OW-M. Our particular aircraft had taken off at approximately 2200 hours from RAF Linton-on-Ouse that night, along with thirteen other Halifaxes, successfully bombing the target area of the railway yards at Louvain. LW682 was one of two No. 426 Squadron Halifaxes lost on this operation on the night of 12/13 May 1944, destined never to return home. Modern-day research can also confirm the names of the young aircrew in LW682 that night.

The five members of the crew whose bodies were all recovered from the wreckage of Halifax LW682 in 1944 were:

*Thomas Wessel Taylor; Flying Officer, navigator, RCAF, of Chisholm Mills, Alta., aged 29.*

*Clifford Stanley Phillips; Flying Officer, bomb aimer, RCAF, of Valparaiso, Sask., aged 25.*

*Jack Edwin McIntyre; Warrant Officer 1st Class, wireless op/gunner, RCAF, of Biggar, Sask., aged 23.*

*Roy Ellerslie; Sergeant, flight engineer, RAFVR, of Doncaster, Yorkshire, aged 37.*

*Joseph Edward Jean Guy Arbour; Flight Sergeant, ventral gunner, RCAF, of Montreal, Que., aged 32.*

In total this left three aircrew unaccounted for:

*Wilbur Boyd Bentz; Flight Sergeant, pilot, RCAF, of Penticton, BC, aged 23.*

*John Wilson Summerhayes; Sergeant, mid-upper gunner, RCAF, of Brantford, Ont., aged 23.*

*Fred Roach, Sergeant; rear gunner, RCAF, of Leamington, Ont., aged 25.*

In 1948 the Belgians awarded the pilot of this crew, Wilbur Boyd Bentz, the Croix de Guerre with palm leaf, in honour of his bravery.

**Right** Parts of the rudder from one of the giant vertical stabilizers.

**Right** Main undercarriage oleo and wheel with shredded tyre attached.

Over the years the crater gradually filled in. Sometimes just the odd spot of iridescent fuel and oil was evident on the surface of the dark water; small bits of twisted metal could also be found by the sharper-eyed observer. Local people knew of the 'bomber in the marsh', and it passed into regional folklore, until, with the increased interest in aviation, the Belgian Aviation History Association

(BAHA) decided to research the incident. It was almost certain that the remains of the missing airmen still lay there, and the feeling was strong that these brave young men should be recovered and given a proper and fitting funeral. During their intensive research BAHA made contact with Jay Hammond, the nephew of the pilot Bentz. Jay had also been doing some exhaustive research, and was extremely interested and excited by the prospect of his uncle's aircraft being excavated, and also by the possibility of a dignified recovery of those crew members who were still missing. It was all too quickly evident that, among all the official permissions and notification required, one massive obstacle would be the financing of such a project. The unearthing from considerable depth of tons of wreckage would not be an economical undertaking, as many aviation archaeologists know only too well.

During the dry summer of 1996 the resultant loss of moisture to the marshy ground enabled BAHA members to conduct a small test excavation by hand. This revealed numerous small fragments of twisted metal and, most poignantly, an RCAF tunic button. During this time BAHA also learned of the efforts of Karl Kjarsgaard, a Canadian who was rebuilding for static display in Trenton a Halifax bomber that had been recovered from a Norwegian lake. Karl was in desperate need of undercarriage assemblies and other parts. Karl quickly realized the potential of the proposed excavation of LW682 and began raising funds. The Canadian Government, the Ministry of Veterans' Affairs and Canadian Heritage all agreed to finance the project. Once all the paperwork had been processed, BAHA began the serious organization and planning for this massive undertaking, and soon the people of Geraardsbergen were also involved. It was not long before the team consisted of over fifty individuals all keen to help. So it was that finally, in September 1997, the site was pumped for two weeks to extract as much water from the area as possible. The Fire Brigade, the National

Guard and the Police were all instrumental in assisting. Then the day came. Also in attendance were two gentlemen, Tony Little and Ed Rae, of the RCAF POW Association; both had flown Halifaxes during the war.

Once the excavator had taken away the surface grass, evidence of burnt soil, tubing, wires and small fragments of twisted metal could be seen almost immediately. The condition overall was very good, and this looked very promising for the Trenton Halifax restoration project. After a few hours, a depth of about 3 metres had been achieved, but suddenly everything had to stop. Quite clearly among the compressed airframe were human remains. Several hours of painstaking respectful recovery then followed, during which the wristwatches of Fred Roach and Jack McIntyre were discovered. Also found were Fred's lighter and a finger ring belonging to Jack. As the search progressed through the still moist clays and sands, the remains of the mid-upper gun turret were found. In among the twisted and crushed framework and shattered Plexiglas were the remains of John Summerhayes, still at his station. His son was called immediately via mobile phone to say that, after so long, his father had been found, and he immediately booked a flight to Belgium. He had never wanted to go to Europe before, knowing that 'somewhere there his father was missing'. Many personal items recovered at this stage were not named, such as a fountain pen, the remains of a wristwatch and a wallet containing some Canadian coins. Since then Cynrik De Decker has done some extensive research and now knows who once actually owned this pen. Another artefact

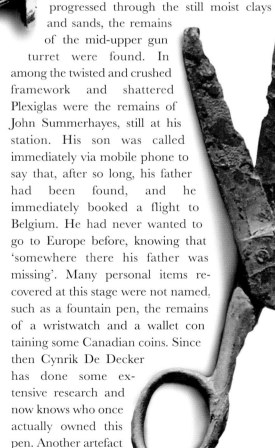

**Left** Another artefact that was identified and whose original owner was established is a wristwatch bezel with face and glass intact. This had once belonged to Warrant Officer 1st Class Jack Edwin McIntyre.

**Below** Close up of scissors, from a medical kit.

The funeral
procession.

**Right** The funeral. In this view, on the left is the coffin and newly prepared headstone of Wilbur Boyd Bentz, aged 23. To the right is the same of Fred Roach, aged 25. Comrades now at peace.

**Right** Also attending the funeral was the sister of Jack Edwin McIntyre, the wireless op/gunner of Halifax LW682 whose body had been recovered and buried back in 1944; he was aged just 23.

that was identified and whose original owner was established was a wristwatch bezel with face and glass intact. This had once belonged to Warrant Officer 1st Class Jack Edwin McIntyre. The recovery of these tiny personal effects exemplified the precision and extensive care with which BAHA conducted this excavation.

Some fourteen hours later, excavation for the day had to finish. So far two Bristol Hercules engines had been recovered, along with landing gear, one with a large tyre still attached, several Browning 0.303 machine guns as well as the ventral Browning 0.50 gun. Parachutes were also located, although only the nylon-manufactured example remained intact. The dinghy, complete with beacon, was also found, as were escape kits containing money and silk maps, survival kits and several massive twisted and broken propeller blades. The next day the excavation continued, and a further Hercules engine was located at a depth of 9 metres . Recovering this was no easy task, as a small tree had grown overhead and had to be removed to access the engine for lifting. The Fire Brigade then assisted in cleaning the masses of compressed wreckage with their power hoses. This was quite some task in itself, as by now the recovery team had unearthed some 7 tons of Halifax.

Meanwhile, back in Canada the preparations were being made to bury the men who had been found. The BAHA insisted that they should be interred along with their colleagues in the Geraardsbergen Cemetery, and local authorities agreed that this was the right thing to do. Finally on

Monday 10 November 1997, the funerals of those who had been missing for so long but were now found took place. The three coffins were escorted by ninety Canadian soldiers; relatives of six of the eight airmen were present, as was the Canadian Minister for Veterans' Affairs, Fred Miflin. Just as the coffins were lowered, three Belgian Marchetti SM260s roared overhead in tribute, flying the 'Missing Man' formation. Among the large crowd of people, an elderly grey-haired gentleman stood as an onlooker. But perhaps onlooker is not the most appropriate word here, for this man had made an incredible, emotional, brave and honourable journey to be here. Eventually this gentleman stepped forward and introduced himself to Jay Hammond. It was Martin Drewes, who wanted to pay his last respects to a fallen foe. Words really are inadequate to describe what happened next and the emotions felt. Several relatives approached Martin Drewes: John Summerhayes's son Doug greeted the man who during a wartime aerial action so long ago had killed his father, while Fred Roach's sister, Mrs Marjorie Wise, held out her hand, and, with typical German politeness, Martin Drewes bent to kiss it. Marjorie then looked at Martin and said 'Can I give you a hug?'

That evening a dinner was held with everyone involved. The relatives were all given personal artefacts with which their next of kin and loved ones had actually been associated. Marjorie could now touch her brother's wristwatch. Mr Taylor, whose brother Tom had been the navigator, received the flight computer. Mrs McIntyre had her brother's wristwatch and finger ring placed into her hands. During the recovery a wallet had been found, but whose was it? Careful examination of the contents revealed two tickets. One was from Nova Scotia, but all the crew had sailed from there. However, the other ticket was from Brantford to Simcoe. This is where John Summerhayes lived. He had

always kept the ticket from his leave to visit his small son. Doug was just 1 year old when his father was killed; fifty-three years later it was Doug's turn to take the ticket home.

Later in November a Canadian C130 Hercules landed at Melsbroek airfield. This aeroplane would undertake a far from normal return flight, as carefully packed in its cargo hold would be sections of Halifax LW682 for the static rebuild Halifax project at Trenton in Canada. One could say that this was indeed the final flight of LW682.

After fifty-three years all the crew were together again. They were complete, resting peacefully alongside each other. How fitting – after all, these young lads had trained, flown, fought and died together. Other sections of LW682 were smelted down into ingots for use at the base of the flag pole at RAF Dishforth. Others will form part of the roof of the loggia of the Royal Air Force Bomber Command memorial to be constructed at the Piccadilly entrance to Green Park in London.

It is arguable that there are no comparable cases involving such complex issues and emotions as the excavation of Halifax LW682 and its three missing crew members. The high levels of dedication, the commitment to succeed, the emotional journeys and the closure for the families of those who had been missing for so long, even though they relate to a period so long ago, are still poignant in today's chaotic world. What indeed would these young men have made of today's world?

Considering all the different aspects of this most remarkable recovery, I really do think that the BAHA and all involved have shown that they have the profound ability to make an aeroplane and its crew 'fly again'. In doing so they have ensured that this crew will never be forgotten. Today we are reminded, as future generations will rightfully be, of the astounding bravery of all Bomber Command aircrews, and of the huge debt owed to them by us all. ●

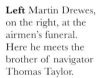

**Left** Martin Drewes, on the right, at the airmen's funeral. Here he meets the brother of navigator Thomas Taylor.

**Below left** Summer 1998. Erwin Van den Broecke (left) and Cynrik De Decker with the ingots, ready for delivery while a Canadian C-130 is waiting on Melsbroek A/B tarmac. These ingots will be used for the Bomber Command memorial in London.

## CHAPTER SEVEN

# OVERLORD SACRIFICE

STEVE DARLOW

RAF BOMBER COMMAND'S CONTRIBUTION TO THE SUCCESS OF THE 1944 D-DAY LAND-INGS APPEARS, TO DATE, TO HAVE BEEN PUBLICLY OVERLOOKED. IN 2009, DURING THE SIXTY-FIFTH ANNIVERSARY CELEBRATIONS OF THE NORMANDY BEACH LANDINGS, THE BRITISH NATIONAL MEDIA COMPLETELY FAILED TO ACKNOWLEDGE WHAT BOMBER COMMAND HAD ACHIEVED IN DIRECT SUPPORT OF OPERATION 'OVERLORD', THE ALLIED RE-ENTRY INTO GERMAN-OCCUPIED WESTERN EUROPE. THE RESPECTIVE AIRCREWS, GROUNDCREWS AND BOMBER COMMAND STATION AND HEADQUARTERS PERSONNEL HAD, IN FACT, PUT UP AN IMMENSE EFFORT. THEY HAD BEEN OPERATING DIRECTLY IN SUPPORT OF THE LANDING FOR THE THREE MONTHS PRIOR TO D-DAY, 6 JUNE 1944, CARRYING OUT A CAMPAIGN OF BOMBING THE RAIL COMMUNICATION NETWORK THAT LED TO NORMANDY, THROUGH WHICH THE GERMANS WOULD HAVE TO MOVE REINFORCEMENTS AND SUPPLIES. FOLLOWING THE ACTUAL NORMANDY D-DAY BEACH ASSAULT, THE BOMBER CREWS CONTINUED WITH THE ATTACKS ON THE RAILYARDS, FRUSTRATING GERMAN DEPLOYMENTS. AT THE TIME THE BOMBER AIRMEN RECEIVED LITTLE RECOGNITION. UNFORTUNATELY LITTLE HAS CHANGED. BUT THOUSANDS OF BOMBER COMMAND AIRCREW LOST THEIR LIVES ENSURING THE SUCCESS OF THE INVASION – A SACRIFICE THAT DESERVED RECOGNITION THEN AND CERTAINLY NOW.

THE RAIL COMMUNICATIONS bombing attacks opened on the night of 6/7 March 1944 with a raid on the Trappes rail facilities. History is now clear in showing that the attacks on the French and Belgian rail targets, through spring 1944 and into the summer, significantly hampered the Germans' ability to respond to the invasion. But this came at a cost, and, in village and town cemeteries all across Normandy, the Somme, Picardy and the Pas de Calais, Commonwealth War Graves headstones mark where Bomber Command airmen now rest, having died in Overlord support operations. This sacrifice was overlooked in the anniversary celebrations; it was also overlooked sixty-five years previously. At the time, Air Chief Marshal Sir Arthur Harris had voiced his concerns to Chief of the Air Staff Sir Charles Portal (on 1 July), stating in a letter: 'I think you should be aware of the full depth of feeling that is being aroused by the lack of adequate or even reasonable credit to the RAF in particular, and the Air Forces as a whole, for their efforts in the Invasion.' Harris went on to quote some statistics.

Up to June 28th in this battle (which is regarded both officially and publicly as mainly a land battle), the British Army has lost some 2,500 killed; the U.S. Army approximately 5,000. In April, May and June which are the three months in which my Command had been engaged almost entirely on invasion work (including the Rocket and Flying Bomb work which must be regarded as part of the invasion war although the casualties on those targets are negligible) my Command alone lost 6,038 killed, wounded and missing. Of those, 5,804 are missing. Of the missing we know from experience only about 20% survive. Therefore my Command alone in this invasion war has suffered nearly 2-times the number killed as the whole of the British Army and more than the U.S. Army…

Yet when it comes to official communiqués and the balancing of publicity the country as a whole and world at large is quite entitled to think that this is almost entirely a land war with the Air Forces doing what they can to assist; whereas in fact they are bearing the brunt.

Harris concluded the letter: 'There are 10,500 air-crew in my operational squadron. In three months we have lost over half that number. They have a right that their story should be adequately told, and it is a military necessity that it should be.'

Bomber Command recorded the accounts of airmen who had initially failed to return from an operation and yet later made their way home, in a 'K' report (Report on Loss of Aircraft on Operations). These records, while matter of fact, provide an invaluable insight into the extraordinary experiences of aircrew and the difficulties and dangers they faced while flying through hostile airspace, under attack, and while trying to get out of a severely damaged aircraft. What follows are three such accounts of Bomber Command airmen 'bearing the brunt'.

On the night of 18/19 April 1944, Bomber Command set a new record, the aircrew flying a total of 1,125 sorties. The majority of sorties were carried out against French rail targets. Almost 1,250 airmen manned the 112 Handley Page Halifaxes, 61 Avro Lancasters and 8 de Havilland Mosquitoes that flew to the rail yards at Noisy-le-Sec. Four Halifaxes would not be returning. There was a total loss of life on three of the aircraft, but on one No. 432 Squadron Halifax one man would eventually be able to tell the tragic circumstances in which some of his Bomber Command colleagues died.

**Left** Across the north of France the Cross of Sacrifice acts as a beacon, in both civil and military cemeteries, indicating the resting place of thousands of Bomber Command airmen who died in direct support of operation Overlord. *(Steve Darlow)*

Report on Loss of Aircraft on Operations

| | | |
|---|---|---|
| Aircraft: | Halifax III No. LW. 643 'E' of No. 432 Squadron | |
| Date of Loss: | 18/19 April 1944 | |
| Target: | Noisy-le-Sec M/Y | |
| Cause of Loss: | Collision | |
| Position of Loss: | Target area | |
| Information from: | Sgt. Shaughnessy G.J. Mid Under Gunner on 14th operation | |

| | | |
|---|---|---|
| Captain & Pilot | P/O Mercer A.C.G. | This crew had completed about 20 operations. |
| Navigator | P/O Bell J.B. | All, except the informant are believed |
| W/Operator | Sgt. Pett S.D. | to be killed. |
| Ft/Engineer | P/O Kent W.H. | |
| Bomb Aimer | F/O Redman A.H. | |
| M/U/Gunner | Sgt. McCluskie A. | |
| R/Gunner | P/O McGregor A.M. | |

Briefed Route: Base - Newbury - Selsey Bill - 4918N 0010W - 4820N 0210E - Target - 4855N 0230E - 4955N 0055E - Reading - Base.

## Narrative:

The informant who was a spare gunner in his squadron had not flown with this crew before. He manned the mid under gun on this occasion. The Halifax took off from East Moor at 2058 hours, crossed the French coast at 13,000 ft. and continued to climb to 15,500 ft. before reaching the target. The night was clear, there being little cloud and visibility was good. The outward flight was uneventful. The Rear Gunner once report- ed that they were being followed by a twin-engined fighter, but the Pilot executed a corkscrew and no attack developed.

On the approach to the target a fire was observed to port probably coming from Juvisy which was also attacked that night. In the target area there was a small amount of flak and many aircraft were seen below the Halifax.

The Halifax made a good bombing run at 15,500 ft. and as far as is known on the briefed heading. The bombs were dropped on T.I.'s. The Bomb Aimer had just called out 'Bombs gone' and the Pilot had not yet made any alteration of course, when there was a terrific crash and informant, who was in the mid lower gun position keeping a look out below was thrown violently about. He was considerably bruised and winded, but not seri- ously hurt. Sgt. Shaughnessy is convinced that the violence of the crash could only be due to a collision with another aircraft, but he never saw the aircraft or heard any warning from any other member of the crew to suggest that a collision was imminent. From the direction of the sound and the damage subsequently observed he believes that the collision must have taken place head on.

The Halifax immediately appeared to turn completely over several times and then went into a steep spiral dive. When Sgt. Shaughnessy recovered his faculties he left his turret intending to put on his parachute. He found that this had been opened and torn in the collision and was unserviceable. With considerable difficulty he made his way forward as far as the front main spar. Passing under the mid upper turret he looked up and noticed that the top of the turret had been broken off. The Gunner appeared to be dead. The Flight Engineer was lying across the main spar unconscious, the Pilot was slumped forward over the controls and the Wireless Operator also appeared to be dead or unconscious. Sgt. Shaughnessy decided that there was nothing he could do to assist them as the whole front part of the aircraft was completely wrecked. There was no sign of fire. Sgt. Shaughnessy then returned to the rear exit and attempted to open it. He man- aged to get it about three quarters open, but then it jammed. He then sought the spare parachute which was kept close by. The side of the fuselage was considerably buckled and the parachute container was badly dented. He was quite unable to extract the para- chute and realised that he could not leave the aircraft. He therefore crouched down on

**Left** Seranvillers-Forenville Military Cemetery. Directly to the right of the Cross of Sacrifice lies Squadron Leader William Stewart and five of his crew. Three headstones record their names and that they lost their lives on the night of 12/13 June 1944.
*(Steve Darlow)*

*Report continued from previous page...*

the floor close to the entrance door awaiting the crash.

The next thing that Sgt. Shaughnessy remembers is being half dragged and half carried along the ground by two German soldiers. They were still within the precincts of the marshalling yard and he noticed two crashed bombers burning nearby. Later he was told that a third had crashed at the other end of the yard. The raid was still in progress and after a few minutes a stick of bombs fell fairly close. The Germans immediately made for safety as fast as they could leaving Sgt. Shaughnessy who escaped in the opposite direction.

O.R.S. Comment: Several reports were received of a collison in the Noisy-le-Sec area on this night.

Canadian Sergeant Shaughnessy would go on to evade capture. One other member of the crew, Sergeant Pett, also survived, and was captured. Canadians Flying Officer Mercer, Pilot Officer Bell and Pilot Officer McGregor, and RAF airmen Pilot Officer Kent, Flying Officer Redman and Sergeant McCluskie all rest in Clichy New Communal Cemetery.

On the night of 6/7 May 1944 Bomber Command sent 149 aircraft and crews to attack the rail facilities at Mantes-La-Jolie (recorded in the Bomber Command records as Mantes-Gassicourt). Three aircraft failed to return, resulting in the loss of ten lives, with seven men evading capture, and four men caught.

## Report on Loss of Aircraft on Operations

| | |
|---|---|
| Aircraft: | Lancaster III No. MD449 'M' of 156 Squadron |
| Date of Loss: | 6/7 May 1944 |
| Target: | Mantes-Gassicourt |
| Cause of Loss: | Fighter |
| Position of Loss: | Conches area |
| Information from: | F/Sgt. Meer G.M.G. Flight Engineer on his 31st operation, F/O Jones P.V. Bomb Aimer on his 38th operation. |

| | | |
|---|---|---|
| Pilot and Captain | F/Lt Churchill H.D. | On his 35th operation Fate unknown |
| Navigator | F/O Foster J.D. | About 35 operations completed Fate unknown |
| Wireless Operator | Sgt. Marle R. | About 35 operations completed Bel. evading |
| Mid Upper Gunner | Sgt. Hayward D.D. | About 35 operations completed Wounded but bel. evading |
| Rear Gunner | F/O Warren D.F. | About 10 operations completed Fate unknown |

The Lancaster took off from Upwood at 0048 on 7th May, set course at 2,000 feet and climbed on track to cross the enemy coast at 10,000 feet. Visibility was excellent and the moon was nearly full.

The crew had been briefed to bomb towards the end of the attack and as the target was approached, the Pilot reported that fighters seemed to be busy over the target area. Bombs were released at the briefed time of 0221 and then, in view of the signs of fighter activity, the Pilot asked the Flight Engineer to come up beside him to keep a look-out.

The route involved a turn to starboard after bombing and holding the new course for about 35 miles before making a 90° turn on to the homeward route. This 90° turn had just been made and the aircraft was flying straight and level at about 9,000 feet when the Rear Gunner reported sighting a suspicious aircraft on the starboard quarter down. He asked the Mid Upper Gunner to watch on the port side and warned the Pilot to prepare for combat. (The Wireless Operator had not reported any suspicious indication on FISH

POND). The Flight Engineer directed his search in the direction indicated by the Gunner and saw a twin-engined aircraft, probably a Ju.88, at a range which he estimated as over 1,000 yards.

The Rear Gunner began to speak again, advising a dive to starboard, but as he spoke, the fighter opened fire and scored hits on the bomber. The Flight Engineer is confident that the range of firing was exceptionally great and estimates it as nearly 1,000 yards.

The details of the damage sustained in this attack are not known precisely but the effect was that GEE and H2S immediately became unserviceable, the Mid Upper Gunner was wounded and the Rear Gunner reported his "guns had gone", but that he was not wounded. The informants believe that cannon fire was responsible as bursts were heard inside the aircraft.

The dive, initiated on the Gunner's warning as the attack began, was carried through steeply and about 4,000 feet of altitude was lost. No sooner was the aircraft levelled out at about 6,000 feet than the Rear Gunner gave warning that the fighter was coming in again from the port quarter. A further dive to 2,000 feet was carried out. The fighter scored no hits in this attack and was engaged by the Mid Upper Gunner

The Pilot began to gain some height but almost immediately the fighter was reported by the Rear Gunner to be coming in again and he decided that, with only the Mid Upper turret available for defence, his best chance of escape lay in going low enough to prevent the fighter from having room to manoeuvre beneath the Lancaster. He therefore dived again and flew on at about 800 feet. The fighter however, attacked repeatedly, usually coming in from the port, i.e. from out of the moon. The only defensive manoeuvre which the Lancaster was able to make was a steep bank and although the fighter did not score hits in every attack, the bomber received some additional damage. The fighter made seven or eight attacks in all. They were made in such rapid succession that informants think it possible that they were assailed by more than one aircraft. Throughout, the Rear Gunner continued to give directions clearly and steadily.

The Bomb Aimer was sent aft to inspect damage and to ascertain the condition of the Rear Gunner. He found that all the visible damage was at the rear of the aircraft and that the Gunner was unhurt.

After the last attack the Pilot reported that he had no rudder control and that the crew should prepare to abandon the aircraft. He added immediately that the aircraft was uncontrollable and told the crew to bale out quickly. The height of the aircraft was then about 700 feet.

The Flight Engineer left first from the front hatch and was followed immediately by the Bomb Aimer. Both pulled their rip cords as they left the aircraft and they both made good descents. They landed rather heavily but unhurt within 50 yards of one another in an open field surrounded by trees. They saw no other parachutes although the Navigator was right behind them as they baled out. The aircraft flew on for about 4 minutes after they left and then hit the ground and burst into flames. A preliminary report received by the informants was that three bodies were found, but the number was later corrected to two.

The place of landing was Le Fidelaire about 30 miles N.W. of Conches.

Flight Lieutenant Churchill, who had been awarded the Distinguished Flying Cross and Bar, lost his life and is buried in Fidelaire Communal Cemetery along with Flying Officer Foster, DFC. Canadian Flying Officer Warren, DFM, is buried in Bretteville-sur-Laize Canadian War Cemetery. The other four men survived to evade capture.

On the night of 12/13 June 1944, Bomber Command sent 671 aircraft to attack communications targets in France, including the railyards at Cambrai. A total of seventeen Halifaxes and six Lancasters failed to return, including the No. 408 Squadron Lancaster flown by Squadron Leader W. B. Stewart.

Report on Loss of Aircraft on Operations

| | |
|---|---|
| Aircraft: | Lancaster II No. DS.726 'Y' of 408 Squadron |
| Date of Loss: | 12/13 June 1944 |
| Target: | Cambrai Railway Junction |
| Cause of Loss: | Fighter attack followed by fire |
| Position of Loss: | Target area |
| Information from: | P/O B.J. La Pierre Gaston Jean Mid Under Gunner on 31st operation |

Remainder of Crew:

| | | |
|---|---|---|
| Captain & Pilot | S/Ldr. Stewart W.B. | All but two believed killed |
| Navigator | F/O Mallory G.E. | |
| W/Operator | P/O Bray J. | |
| F/engineer | Sgt. Varley H. | |
| Air Bomber | F/O Burns W.C. | |
| M/U/Gunner | P/O Ochsner R.D. | |
| Rear Gunner | W/O Murphy H.F. | |

Route: Base - Flamborough - Docking - Sheerness - Dungeness - 4955N 0113E - 4953N 0205E - Target - 5012N 0322E - 5036N 0252E - 5108N 0240E - Orfordness.

Narrative: The Lancaster took off from Linton-on-Ouse at about 2200 hours. The French coast was crossed at about 5,000 ft. and the sortie was normal as far as the target area. The weather was fairly clear with starlight but no moon.

The target was reached at 2355 hours, and the Lancaster made a run across the target, but the Air Bomber missed the T.I. markers. During this run the Mid Under Gunner saw an Me.110 pass below from astern to ahead. The Pilot turned to begin a second run, for which the Air Bomber was giving him directions. The Mid Under Gunner was throwing out WINDOW when he suddenly heard the Rear Gunner firing. Looking round he saw an Me.110, about 300 yds, below and astern, at which the Rear Gunner was firing. The Mid Under Gunner turned his gun round and saw his tracer strike the cockpit of the enemy aircraft which he believed was shot down.

The Lancaster was hit about the nose, in front of the bomb-bay and near the root of the port wing. Informant stated the strikes were M/G fire, not cannon. The port inner tank caught fire at once and the flames streaming back, enveloped the Mid Under Gunner's turret. The aircraft was now diving steeply and the Pilot gave the order to bale out. The Mid Under Gunner helped the Mid Upper Gunner to get out of his turret which was rendered difficult by the aircraft's acceleration. Flames were now entering the fuselage and the Mid Under Gunner baled out from his turret (pushing the M/Gs aside). His parachute worked normally and he made a good landing at midnight at Riemilly, south of Cambrai. He noticed one other 'chute descending.

Information was told afterwards that the aircraft had crashed on a German airfield nearby and that there were five bodies on board; also that one German fighter had been shot down.

On the Cambrai raid, nine aircraft were lost: forty-two men lost their lives, eleven men were captured, and fourteen men evaded capture. Canadian Squadron Leader Stewart was one of those who lost his life, along with fellow Canadians Flying Officer Mallory, Pilot Officer Ochsner and Warrant Officer Murphy. RAF airmen Sergeant Varley and Pilot Officer Bray similarly did not survive. The six airmen who died now rest in Seranvillers-Forenville Military Cemetery. Canadian Flying Officer Burns was captured and Canadian Pilot Officer La Pierre evaded capture and was able to provide the information from which the 'K' report was produced. ●

German Air Ministry report, 13 June 1944, describing the effect of the Allied bombing attacks on rail communications.

The raids carried out in recent weeks have caused the breakdown of all main lines; the coastal defences have been cut off from the supply bases in the interior, thus producing a situation which threatens to have serious consequences. Although even the transportation of essential supplies for the civilian population have been completely stopped for the time being and only the most vital military traffic is moved, large scale strategic movement of German troops by rail is practically impossible at the present time and must remain so while attacks are maintained at their present intensity.

## CHAPTER EIGHT

# INTO THE SILENCE

ADAM PURCELL

AS THE SECOND WORLD WAR PROGRESSED, YOUNG MEN FROM ALL OVER THE WORLD TOOK UP ARMS, OFTEN CROSSING CONTINENTS AND OCEANS, TO FIGHT NAZISM. RECRUITS FROM THE BRITISH COMMONWEALTH WOULD LEAVE FAMILIES BEHIND TO FIGHT A EUROPEAN WAR. TRAGICALLY MANY WOULD NOT RETURN, INCLUDING JUST OVER 4,000 AUSTRALIANS WHO WERE SERVING WITH THE ROYAL AUSTRALIAN AIR FORCE AS PART OF ROYAL AIR FORCE BOMBER COMMAND. THEIR WRITTEN WORDS, PHOTOGRAPHS SNAPPED WHEN THE OPPORTUNITY AROSE AND OFFICIAL CORRESPONDENCE ARE ALL THAT MANY RELATIVES NOW HAVE TO REMEMBER WHAT THESE MEN DID, WHAT THEY WENT THROUGH AND WHY THEY FAILED TO RETURN.

Aloft in a Tiger Moth in late August 1939, Gilbert Firth Pate experienced flight for the first time. The 23-year-old Australian circled above his family home in Kogarah, New South Wales, with a pilot friend, shortly after take-off from Mascot aerodrome in Sydney. Perhaps that first flight had impressed him. Days later war was declared. Pate, like many others, would eventually make application to the Royal Australian Air Force.

Gilbert was the only son in the Pate family, following older sisters Kittie and Peggy. His father, Sydney Firth Pate, was originally from Padiham, Lancashire, in the UK. Kathleen Upton, his mother, was from Windsor, north-west Sydney. The family were in Caulfield, Victoria, when Gilbert was born in August 1916. After the birth of their fourth child, a daughter named Joyce, in 1930, the Pate family moved to Sydney, NSW. When his schooling had finished when he was aged 17, Gilbert began working as a strapper at the local stables near the family home in Bown's Road, Kogarah. He briefly trained as a jockey, but the staunchly anti-gambling Sydney Pate put a stop to that after Gilbert won his first and only race by sixteen lengths.

It was in September 1940, while working as a wool classifier at Commonwealth Wool & Produce, that Pate applied for aircrew. While waiting he served as a sapper with the Anti Aircraft Search Light branch of the Australian army between January and March 1941. Gilbert married Edith Grace Cox (known as Grace) on 13 June 1942. A photo, undated and believed to have been taken at Manly in Sydney, shows the two of them strolling along the promenade. Gilbert finally began his Air Force career exactly one week after his marriage.

Most of Pate's Air Force training took place in Australia: Bradfield Park, Sydney NSW; Parkes, country NSW; Port Pirie, South Australia. He was awarded his air gunner's badge on 4 March 1943. He took five days' leave at home, before waiting at No. 2 Embarkation Depot, Bradfield Park, for a ship to war. His family says that that was the last time he saw them or visited Grace. The ship sailed from Brisbane, destination unknown, on 20 April 1943.

It appears that the prospect of sailing to the other side of the world inspired Gilbert to begin what would become a prolific output of letters. The first, dated 6 May 1943 is headed, 'LETTER 1'. 'Dear Mum', it begins. 'This letter is being written after being at sea for 16 days, so far we haven't seen any land + don't expect to until we reach a port we have been to before.' Under wartime censorship, this would appear to have been a reference to San Francisco, where the Pate family had lived for a short while in the 1920s. A postcard to sister Joyce was sent on 10 May 1943 from Salt Lake City, which suggests that Gilbert travelled across America via what Hank Nelson called 'the northern line', across the Rocky Mountains and on to Chicago.

It is clear from his letters that Gilbert thoroughly enjoyed his fortnight in the United States. 'The idea of bars being open until 12 pm for 7 days a week seems a very good idea as I haven't seen more than an isolated case of drunkenness since my arrival,' he wrote to his mother on 19 May. 'I have sampled

**Left** 'Large and Small' – Sydney Pate and his son Gilbert. Probably taken around 1920, when Gilbert was four years old. *(Gil and Peggy Thew)*

**Right** Gilbert Pate shortly after joining the Royal Australian Air Force. The white flash in his cap indicates that he was in training when this photograph was taken. *(Gil and Peggy Thew)*

quite a bit of good food since I have been on leave [in Rhode Island]. Pancakes with maple syrup + fried chicken, strawberries + ice cream… I am taking advantage of the shortage which will be my lot in the very near future.' He later wrote to a cousin of his father's named Raymond Smith: 'I found America very much like home + the New England folks certainly gave us a swell time. I could quite easily settle there permanently.' A photograph was taken of Gilbert in uniform on 16 May. Other photos from the same day show him with three other airmen, each with a young woman on their arm.

By the end of May, after his brief spell of leave, Gilbert was once again at sea. This time the trip was not as pleasant.

The weather is becoming colder when we go up on deck, but everything is very quite [sic] + so far nothing has been seen of the submarine wolf pack which is supposed to haunt these parts. Our boys have a submarine watch to do + we take turns in going on the bridge to keep a lookout.

Gilbert disembarked at Glasgow and went to 11 Personnel Dispatch and Reception Centre (PDRC),

Brighton, England. There, from the window of his billet, he watched aircraft flying across the water towards France. At night, he could see the flashes of the coastal guns firing across the Channel.

Pate had left Australia a fully qualified air gunner, but his training was not over yet. He was posted to No. 17 Operational Training Unit (OTU) at RAF Silverstone; there were only four other Australians there when he arrived on 22 June 1943. Flying became a recurring theme in Gilbert's letters: 'I have done a couple of weeks ground school as a refresher + the last two weeks have been flying in Wellingtons,' he wrote to Joyce from RAF Silverstone on 18 July. 'Flying over here is quite nice all the countryside is under cultivation + it looks just like a billiard table from the air.' In August he wrote to his mother: 'I am seeing a good deal of the country by air. I have taken in a good bit of England + Wales + part of Scotland + the Isle of Man, it's one way of getting around when time is limited.'

In his letters Gilbert initially avoided talk of any apprehension he might have felt at impending operations. The language on one occasion suggests he was trying to stay positive: 'I should be seeing most of Europe by the middle of October, may even go to Italy for the picnic.' But there was no doubt he knew combat operations were getting closer. The fate of Gilbert's flying logbook is unknown, so it is difficult to confirm an exact date, but his first sortie over enemy-held territory – a 'Nickel' or leaflet-dropping operation often used as a 'gentle' introduction for crews nearing the end of their operational training – probably occurred from RAF Silverstone. 'I was on a sortie over Paris recently', he wrote on 20 August, 'but things went off smoothly.'

There was some respite, however. Like many Australian aircrew, Pate had family in England. His uncle Herbert still lived in Padiham, Lancashire. After completing his OTU course at RAF Silverstone, Gilbert spent a week with him. 'I am writing this from Padiham where I have been since Aug 27th. I have been miles since my arrival + nearly all by Shank's ponies, it's marvellous where these people get their energy from,' he wrote to Kathleen. Another letter described how he had caught a

**Left** Grace and Gilbert Pate. Photograph appears to have been taken in Manly, Sydney. *(Gil and Peggy Thew)*

**Right** Sergeant
Gilbert Firth Pate,
RAAF. Photograph
is dated 16 May 1943,
which places it while
Gilbert was travelling
across the United
States en route to war.
*(Gil and Peggy Thew)*

At the end of September Pate and his crew were at a heavy conversion unit at RAF Winthorpe, near Newark, the final step before an operational squadron. Meanwhile, friends and acquaintances were beginning to get into action – and some were not returning: 'The chap who took those snaps I sent you of our trip through the USA is missing, also one of my friends in the pictures we had taken … has been killed.' With the spectre of thirty operational flights now looming large, Gilbert's letters became a little more pensive. 'I will be commencing operations almost immediately,' he wrote to Kathleen on 30 October, 'and hope my luck holds out… Am missing you + Grace very much + would like just 10 minutes at home to see you all.'

Pate and his crew – captained by a Pilot Officer J. E. W. Teager – arrived at No. 49 Squadron at RAF Fiskerton on 22 October 1943. On 3 November, Pate was on the battle order for an operation to Düsseldorf, filling in for an injured rear gunner with a different crew. Pilot Officer Teager flew as second pilot with an experienced crew to gain some operational familiarity before taking his own crew into battle. Pate returned safely – but Teager did not. He was shot down and spent the rest of the war as a prisoner. Pate's crew had lost their pilot before they had even flown a trip together. 'It seems hard to realise,' he wrote, 'until the empty bed space tells its tales.'

Curiously, Gilbert visited a fortune teller in November 1943: 'She says I'll be out of the Service by next May, not long to wait is it?' he asked Joyce. Perhaps this was an attempt to make sense of the topsy-turvy world in which he found himself.

After the loss of Teager, Pate's crew was given a new pilot, a Canadian who had survived a flying accident and was just returning to operations. The pilot had been badly affected by the accident, however, and after a month 'his nerves began to play up so he was taken from us'. Once more without a pilot, the crew was broken up and scattered around various squadrons. Pate found himself posted to the crew of an Australian, Squadron Leader D. P. S. (Phil) Smith. He considered his new pilot 'quite a nice chap who has already completed one tour of ops and may God spare him for a second'.

Gilbert described the 'other bods' on his crew in a letter to Kathleen and Joyce in April 1944: 'an

train and bus to Herbert's home, spending the day walking the village and meeting many people who had known his father Sydney. 'Many remembered him or his doings as if they had taken place the day previously, instead of nearly half a century ago,' he wrote. 'Apart from a few factories I don't think this village has ever changed + it never will…'

Other times, Gilbert travelled to the capital. 'London holds no terrors for me + I find my way damn near anywhere,' he wrote in April 1944. 'Of course the reason for spending leaves in London is because the boys who are still pottering about make it a kind of general meeting ground.' Gilbert also visited a cousin of his mother's during one leave, in October 1943. Albert Farrow and his wife Emily lived in Kensington. Their young grandson was later to be posted missing over Germany. Though he had an offer to stay with the Farrows, Gilbert elected to stay at the Victoria League Club, because 'I don't like to feel tied down.'

Aust. Navigator Jack Purcell from Strathfield + another Aust. Wireless operator from Brisbane, "Pepper Johnston". The other 3 boys are English lads.' They were bomb aimer Jerry Parker from Lancashire, mid-upper gunner Eric Hill, Berkshire and flight engineer Ken Tabor, Bournemouth. All seven were posted to No. 467 Squadron, RAF Waddington, on the last day of 1943.

Squadron Leader Smith had taken over as Flight Commander, 'A' Flight, and the extra administration associated with that role meant that he and his crew would not fly as frequently as ordinary squadron crews might. Pate in fact went to London on leave early in January – where he had a formal portrait taken. Hair perfectly combed and air gunner's badge prominent on his uniform jacket, he signed the photograph 'Love Gil', dated it 5.1.44 and sent it to his mother. Also around this time he learned of his promotion to Flight Sergeant, which had been backdated to September. Gilbert's first operation with No. 467 Squadron was to Berlin on 28 January 1944.

It is interesting to note that Gilbert made no mention in any of his letters until almost the end of February that he was now flying on operations regularly – by which time he had completed four trips. Instead, he wrote of more mundane, homely things: receiving packages of food from his mother and newspapers from his father, talking about the weather and asking about the family. '[I] have gained a little weight,' he wrote on 1 February, 'am now about 10st but getting a few crows feet around the eyes as you will notice by the photograph I sent you. I'll be 28 shortly guess it seems a long time to you.'

By this time the Battle of Berlin was in full swing, and losses were high. On 28 January, 683 aircraft were dispatched to the 'Big City'; 43 were reported missing (6.3 per cent). On 15 February, 891 aircraft were sent and 42 went missing (4.7 per cent). Clearly the scale of losses in this period did not give confidence to an airman facing a tour of thirty operations. 'I have been twice to Berlin + expect to go again to finish it off, so far we have had fairly good trips,' Gilbert wrote to Kathleen on 22 February. He would return there once more before the end of March. He sent Grace and his father newspaper cuttings covering some of the operations on which he took part, perhaps preferring to leave the details to the press. Certainly the language used in the newspaper reports was always positive.

**Left** Four Australian airmen with American women, 16 May 1943. Gilbert Pate is fourth from the right.
*(Gil and Peggy Thew)*

**Failed to return
on 10 May 1944.**
From left to right:
Sergeant Eric
Reginald Hill, RAF,
mid upper gunner,
Flight Sergeant
Gilbert Firth Pate,
RAAF, rear gunner,
Sergeant Kenneth
Harold Tabor, RAF,
flight engineer, Flight
Sergeant Alistair Dale
Johnston, RAAF,
wireless operator,
Squadron Leader
Donald Philip Smeed
Smith, DFC, RAAF,
pilot, Warrant Officer
Royston William
Purcell, RAAF,
navigator, Flight
Sergeant Jeremiah
Parker, RAF, bomb
aimer. *(Adam Purcell)*

'Munich and Karlsruhe, deep inside Germany, were still burning yesterday after Bomber Command's great attack during Monday night', reads one article from the *Daily Mail* of 26 April 1944. 'Only 29 bombers were lost, a percentage very much below the average.' Gilbert's handwriting appears at the top of the page: 'Munich was my target + 10 hrs is a lifetime in the air.'

As he moved further into his operational tour Gilbert's letters occasionally contained indications that he knew exactly how low his chances of survival were. 'So far I have managed to keep out of trouble for which I am extremely thankful,' he wrote to Kathleen on 17 March 1944. 'Second chances don't come very often.' He also had some sad news about airmen he had flown with: 'Two of the boys of the first crew drew the crow [i.e. experienced an outstanding piece of bad luck] on Stuttgart, still that's all in the game.' By the end of the war, just one of the seven men in the Teager crew from No. 49 Squadron survived untouched. One other was a prisoner – the other five were dead.

Despite this, Pate still felt that he lived comfortably, two to a room above the Sergeants' Mess at RAF Waddington, with hot water and central heating. Cakes and comfort parcels arrived regularly from his family. Above all, he knew he was not slogging it out with the infantry: 'Things aren't to [sic] bad over here + when I see the "newsreels" of the fighting in New Guinea + Italy I think I am quite well off.'

The Battle of Berlin is generally considered to have concluded with the operation on 24 March 1944. That was Pate's twelfth trip. Almost a week later, he took part in the infamous operation to Nuremburg that claimed ninety-five bombers. While big cities in Germany such as Essen, Schweinfurt and Munich remained as targets, from mid-April the focus of the assault shifted. Attacks on French targets began to take prominence in preparation for the D-Day landings. Pate flew to places such as Juvisy (18 April) and La Chapelle (20 April), both operations part of a pre-invasion strategy called the Transportation Plan. Designed by Deputy Supreme Commander of the Allied Expeditionary Force, Sir Arthur Tedder, the plan called for 'the destruction of thirty-seven railway centres in France, Belgium and western Germany,

and especially of the locomotive depots and repair and maintenance facilities in these places, in order to prevent the flow of reinforcements and supplies for the German army in the invasion area.' It was in this context that, on 10 May 1944, Pate and his crew were briefed for an operation to marshalling yards at Lille in northern France. Flying in Lancaster Mk III B for Baker, serial LM475 (which had become the crew's usual aircraft), they took off from RAF Waddington at 2157 hours. Wireless signals were received from the aircraft at 2330 hours and at 2345 hours. Beyond that, there was nothing.

In Sydney, at 9.20 a.m. on 16 May 1944, Grace Pate's mother, Mrs Cox, was handed a telegram for Grace: 'REGRET TO INFORM YOU THAT YOUR HUSBAND FLIGHT SERGEANT GILBERT FIRTH PATE IS MISSING AS RESULT OF AIR OPERATIONS ON 11TH MAY 1944 STOP…'

Gilbert's wife, Grace, was listed as his next of kin. Consequently Sydney and Kathleen did not receive direct notification from the Air Force that their son had been posted missing. Grace delivered the news in person. When this happened is not recorded, but it is clear that Kathleen in particular was not happy that she had been left to hear the news second hand. Sydney wrote a protesting letter to the Air Force on 23 May. Uncharacteristically, the letter is not in his usual flowing handwriting, but is typed: 'I respectfully submit one request for your favourable consideration, and it is to ask if you can notify my wife, Mrs Kathleen Pate, 17 Bown's Road, Kogarah, N.S.W. simultaneously with any communications to my son's wife.' After Grace had also written to the Air Force to clarify the situation a few days later, she received a reply dated 7 June 1944. The Air Force handled the situation with sympathetic but firm composure: 'This Department has agreed to keep your husband's parents fully informed of any news which may be sent to you in the future, but this will not affect your position in any way.' The file of correspondence at the National Archives of Australia contains two copies of all further communications regarding Gilbert – one each for Grace and Kathleen.

There was very little information forthcoming from official sources regarding what might have happened to Gilbert and his crew. It fell to the

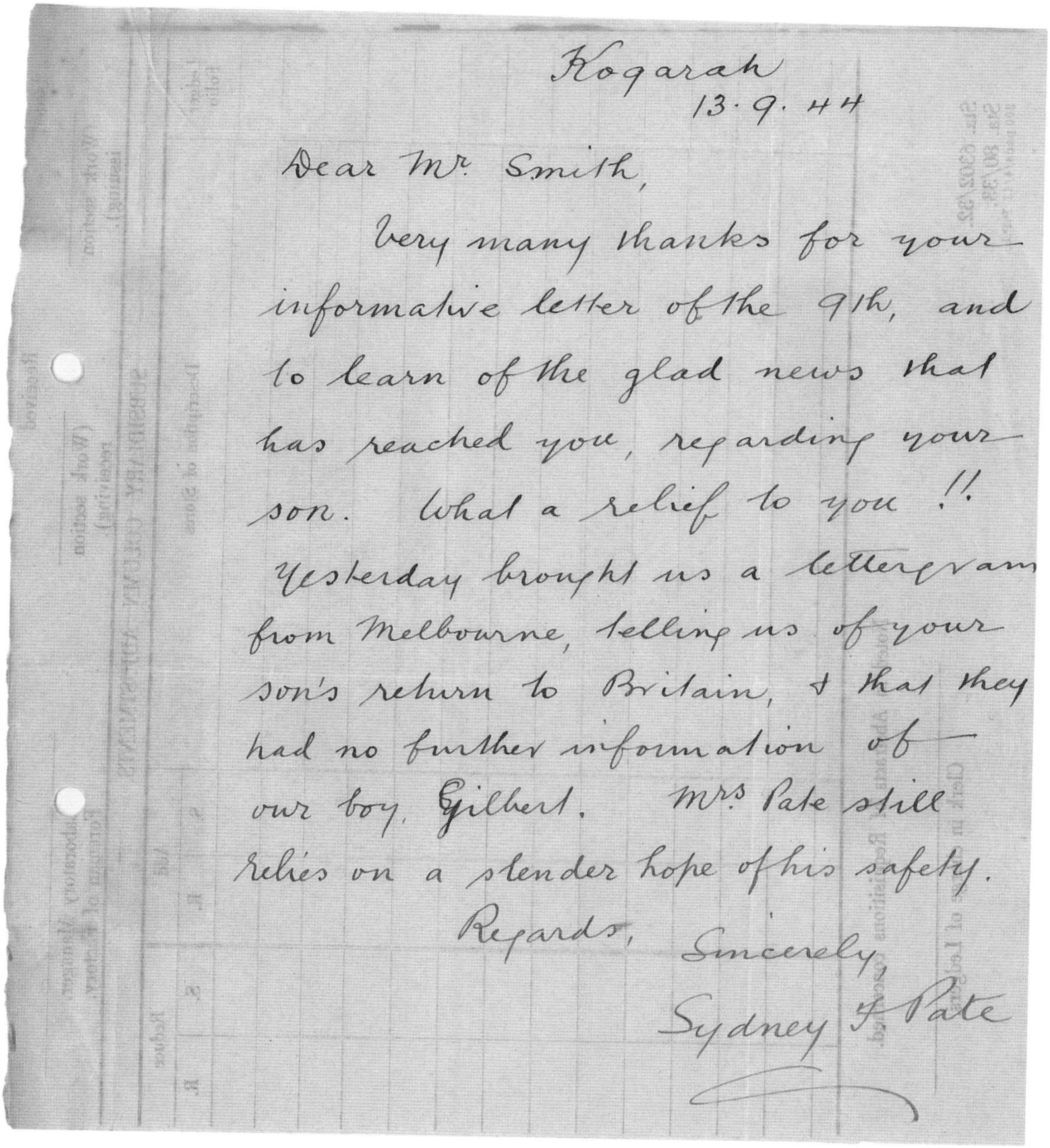

Kogarah
13·9·44

Dear Mr Smith,

very many thanks for your informative letter of the 9th, and to learn of the glad news that has reached you, regarding your son. What a relief to you !!

Yesterday brought us a lettergram from Melbourne, telling us of your son's return to Britain, & that they had no further information of our boy, Gilbert. Mrs Pate still relies on a slender hope of his safety.

Regards,
Sincerely,
Sydney F Pate

**Left** Letter, Sydney Pate to Don Smith, 13 September 1944. *(Reproduced by courtesy of Mollie Smith)*

families themselves to try and make as much sense of it as they could. Don Smith – father of Gilbert's pilot Squadron Leader Smith – obtained addresses for the Australian families through the Air Force and wrote to each. So began a rich correspondence between Don Smith and Sydney Pate. About a dozen of Sydney's letters remain in the superb archive belonging to Mollie Smith, widow of Phil Smith, dated between July 1944 and February 1945. Sydney passed on to Don extracts from the newspaper articles that Gilbert had sent him. He asked his brother Herbert in Lancashire to visit the wife of Jerry Parker, the bomb aimer in Gilbert's crew, and offered to report back to Don when he heard from Herbert following the visit. 'Every day I wonder + cogitate about what really happened to the Lancaster on May 10/11,' he wrote to Don in August 1944. 'It's such a peculiar happening – into the silence.'

On 2 August 1944, advice was received that 'your

son, Flight Sergeant Gilbert Firth Pate, previously reported missing… is now reported missing but believed to have lost his life.' Five days later, a telegram confirmed the death of Jerry Parker. Hope now seemed gone. But on 11 September, a light appeared in the darkness: 'ADVICE RECEIVED THAT ONE AUSTRALIAN MEMBER OF YOUR SON'S CREW SQUADRON LEADER D.P.S. SMITH HAS ARRIVED SAFELY IN THE UNITED KINGDOM STOP CREW CONSISTED OF SEVEN MEMBERS…'

Sydney immediately wrote to Don Smith: 'What a relief to you!' As well as raising hopes that Gilbert might also have survived, this news presented the

possibility of finding out, from someone who was there, what had happened to the aeroplane on that fateful night in May. But it was not to be. Squadron Leader Smith's first letter to his parents after his liberation revealed very little: 'All I can say about the accident is that I was extremely lucky to get away with it. I had a seat type parachute and fell clear whereas the others had observer types and I cannot hold out any hopes for them.'

Sydney Pate wrote about this to Don Smith in October 1944: 'I am struck by [Philip's] use of the word 'accident', its precise application is still not clear to me… was it from enemy attack? Was it from internal misadventure? Was it from its own bomb load?'

Even Phil Smith himself never knew exactly what caused his aircraft to crash. 'We were just about to drop our bombs when everything went hot and dry and red,' he wrote years after the war in an unpublished typescript.

'When the flame had gone out, I was still in my seat but could feel no aeroplane about me. I immediately released my seatbelts and then my parachute…' Phil would shelter with a French family in a small country village. He was liberated when the invasion forces passed in September 1944, returned to the UK and was eventually repatriated to Australia.

The next letter to the Pates from the Air Force was dated 24 October 1944: 'I greatly regret that advice has been received from the Air Ministry, London, quoting French information which states that your son's place of burial is the Cemetery at Lezennes, in the Department of Nord, France, in grave No. 2.' The matter was placed beyond doubt when some photographs of the funeral procession emerged from the Air Force in late 1945. In the end, Gilbert's fortune teller had been right. By May 1944, he was indeed out of the Service – in the most heartbreaking way possible.

**Right** Formal portrait of Gilbert Pate, taken while on leave in London, 5 January 1944. *(Gil and Peggy Thew)*

**Left** Funeral procession, Lezennes, France, May 1944. A clandestine photograph taken by a French civilian and passed on to the Pate family by the RAAF. *(Gil and Peggy Thew)*

For Kathleen Pate, Gilbert's death was particularly difficult. 'As you infer, Time is a great healer,' wrote Sydney Pate to Don Smith in September 1944, 'but I'm sure it will be a long time before my wife takes a normal interest in everyday affairs.' Peggy Thew (née Pate) remembers her mother turning the house at Bown's Road into a virtual mausoleum: 'She walked along the house all day long. She really outdid Queen Victoria in the mourning stakes.'

Kathleen became quite resentful of Grace, who by 1946 had remarried. The Air Force told her in that year that Gilbert's service medals would be forwarded to Grace. Devastatingly for Kathleen, who had already been issued with a Female Relative's Badge and a Mother's and Widow's Badge, 'It is regretted that no other form of recognition of your late son's service is available for issue to you.'

In a letter on 27 October 1944, Sydney Pate wrote to Don Smith about the recent news of Gilbert's place of burial: 'Mrs Pate says she won't rest until she has suitable opportunity to get there.' As it happened, only Kittie ever visited the grave, in November 1954. 'It is a lovely peaceful setting with a hedge round it + set in fields,' she wrote to her parents and Joyce. 'Placed some flowers for you.'

Some of those flowers she pressed and sent home with the letter. Carefully wrapped in yellowing tissue paper, they still sit in the box that holds Gilbert's effects.

Gilbert's nephew, Gil Thew, was the next known member of the family to visit Lezennes, in 1979. Gil says that he was always very aware of the story of his uncle while growing up. He shares his name. Sadly, this appears to have been the source of some antipathy shown to him by Kathleen, who never quite coped after losing her son. For Gil, whose father had been a signaller in Borneo during the war, growing up meant being exposed to gatherings of his father's army mates, where conversation would revolve around the war – the mud and the footslogging and the 'boredom of 45 months of training and sitting around followed by 25 days of sheer terror' fighting the Japanese at Tarakan. Gilbert Pate, on the other hand, is still seen as 'extremely dashing', as an almost romantic hero.

Today, a row of distinctive white Commonwealth War Graves sits in the communal cemetery in Lezennes. The town has encroached so that the cemetery is no longer set in fields, but it remains a peaceful place. ●

## CHAPTER NINE

# 'LOVE AND REMEMBRANCE LAST FOR EVER'

## STEVE DARLOW

AT HALF PAST THREE ON THE MORNING OF 27 AUGUST 1944, THE RESIDENTS OF THE SMALL DANISH VILLAGE OF ÅSTRUPLUND WERE AWOKEN BY THE SOUND OF AN INTENSE AIR BATTLE TAKING PLACE IN THE NIGHT SKIES ABOVE THEIR HOMES. THOSE WHO GAZED INTO THE NIGHT HAD THEIR FACES ILLUMINATED AS A FIREBALL FLASHED OVERHEAD, PLUMMETING INTO A FIELD OUTSIDE THE VILLAGE. THE FIREBALL WAS IN FACT AN AVRO LANCASTER MANNED BY FOUR BRITISH AND THREE CANADIAN AIRMEN. THE ROYAL AIR FORCE HEAVY BOMBER DISINTEGRATED IN A BALL OF FLAME IN THE FIELD OF FARMER SVEND ANDERSEN, WHO, LATER THAT MORNING, MADE HIS WAY TO THE CRASH SITE, GUARDED AND CORDONED OFF BY GERMAN SOLDIERS. SVEND PERSUADED ONE OF THOSE SERVING IN THE ARMY THAT OCCUPIED HIS COUNTRY TO ALLOW HIM CLOSER TO SEE IF THERE HAD BEEN MUCH DAMAGE TO HIS CROPS. THE HORROR OF WHAT HE SAW REMAINED WITH HIM FOR THE REST OF HIS LIFE.

THOUSANDS OF CANADIANS answered the call to take up arms and fight a war across an ocean in Europe. Tens of thousands of those who put their names forward for duty with the Royal Canadian Air Force went on to serve with RAF Bomber Command in the air offensive against Nazism. Those left at home followed the progress of the war via the national press and the radio and some maybe even recognized familiar faces on the newsreels. The personal details of husbands, sons and brothers, however, usually came via the written word, often taking weeks if not months to arrive, though some of the unwelcome correspondence would arrive more quickly.

The letters of John Ernest Fitzgerald are typical of those written by young Canadian airmen serving with RAF Bomber Command in the United Kingdom, portraying his keenness to make a contribution for the cause he had signed up for, and describing his frustrations with the delays in training. On 19 February 1944 Jack, training as an air gunner, wrote to his mother and 'Ruth'.

For the last three days I have been trying to get in a little flying time but everything seems to be against me. Either my pilot's sick or the aircraft is unserviceable. It is starting to get me down because I'm just itching to get flying again… For the last three days I haven't done a thing except sit around and clean the occasional gun. This monotony is beginning to get me down. As you can plainly see I can't think of a darn thing to write about, but I guess you will be glad to know that I am still alive and kicking at everything and everybody… One of these days I will write a decent letter that is if anything exciting ever happens that I can write about. Well I will sign off now. Lots of Love, Jack.

Jack wrote on 'May 1 I think' to 'My Dearest Mother & Sister.' 'Hello sweethearts how is my two best girl friends coming along?' Jack mentioned a visit he had made to Westminster Abbey:

an immensely high place. It must be around three hundred feet from the floor to the ceiling. Inside it smells musty as though a lot of books were slowly

crumbling into dust. There are statues of famous artists and there work all over the place and the actually coffins of the people. Under the floor are graves of people who did a few famous deeds in their life. I didn't notice any Fitzgeralds or Mills there though. Probably we were there under an assumed name though. About the most striking place of all was the grave of the unknown soldier, it impressed me deeply for some reason or other … we went a walk in St James Park near the Buckingham Palace. It was a swell place and what I liked was the fact that they had Mallard ducks tearing around the place. It sure reminded me of the good old days when I used to go hunting with Uncle Frank. I would have liked to have the old trusty 12 gauge and made our fine feathered friends a nice roast duck. All I could see when I saw them swimming around was one of your good old roast duck dinners on the hoof.

Owing to the fact that Bomber Command was fully engaged in operations directly supporting the build-up to the Normandy invasion, many sorties were

**Left** John Ernest Fitzgerald. *(Unless indicated all images the Fitzgerald family via the Canadian Letters and Images Project)*

**Above** Believed to be a trainee colleague of Jack's. Written on the back is, 'To Jack – the best Canuck I ever met. Bill'.

*as one sortie. The result is that some aircrews must inevitably finish their operational tour having experienced far less risk and strain than others, which is obviously undesirable. In addition, with the large amount of bombing of targets in France and occupied territory now being or about to be undertaken, crews will finish their operational tours too quickly, and the crew strength of squadrons cannot possibly be maintained… In view of the above I consider it essential to differentiate between the two entirely different types of operation, and to institute two separate methods of assessing operational sorties. I have therefore given instructions that bombing and minelaying operations which are carried out in an area W of 7°E and N of 53°N, and W of 6°E between 53°N and 46°N should each be counted as one third of a sortie only.)*

Such a policy, unsurprisingly, did not go down too well with aircrew. In a letter of 18 May Jack, yet to take part in main force operations, mentioned the new Bomber Command policy.

My Dearest Mother & Sister
Well Mom I feel pretty low for not writing more often. But I have really been working for the last few weeks. When we got off leave we went right on to an advanced gunnery school and they worked us twenty-four hours a day. But it was really worth it. Cause we were really taught some good stuff. My mid upper gunner and myself both made 89% in our final exams, which I think is pretty good.

That raid I had over France. I don't know whether it counts or not. Some say it does and some say it doesn't so I don't know what to think. By the way Gene has now made 18 trips which is pretty good in a way and pretty lousy in a way because he has been doing these targets in France and each trip consists of only 1/3 of a op. which is silly because if you go over there and get killed you don't get only 1/3 killed. Jack

of shorter duration over French and Belgian territory, rather than the more distant German raids. Bomber Command began to record these as less than a full operation in terms of contributing to the main force tally of thirty operations for a complete tour.

*(Commander-in-Chief of Bomber Command Air Chief Marshal Sir Arthur Harris dispatch 8 March 1944: The risk, fatigue and strain in respect of operations carried out against short range and lightly defended targets in France, and short range mining operations where fighter defence is practically nil, is nowadays in no way comparable to those associated with long range targets in Germany. Under present arrangements those entirely different types of operation count*

Having been posted to No. 166 Squadron in the middle of June 1944, Jack and his crew flew their first operational sortie on the night of 27/28 June – an attack on the V1 flying bomb launch site at Château Bernapré. Since mid-June hundreds of flying bombs had flown low across the English Channel, fired from launch sites in northern

France, and aimed at London. The toll of civilian casualties had steadily risen. Bomber Command had been tasked with lowering the V1 launch rates, attacking the launch sites and the supply and storage organization. These were short raids, but there was still danger. On the night of 27/28 June the No. 166 Squadron Lancaster of Pilot Officer Hunt, DFC, was lost, with no survivors. Jack continued to play his part in the V1 counter-offensive,

with raids to Domleger (29 June and 2 July), Oisemont (30 June) and then also the V2 rocket site at Wizernes on 20 July. In between there were raids supporting the Normandy land battle, notably on Caen on 7 July and Sannerville on 18 July, Bomber Command having been called in to blast an opening for the Allied land forces attempting to break open the front lines. Bomber Command also maintained attacks on rail targets bringing supplies to the German forces; Jack was involved in raids to Orleans on the night of 4/5 July and Revigny on 12/13 July and 14/15 July. Twenty Lancasters were lost on these raids; five from No. 166 Squadron on the Revigny attacks. Then there were the continuing attacks on German targets: Scholven/Buer oil plant on 18/19 July, Kiel (23/24 July), Stuttgart (25/26 and 27/28 July). Against the last of these raids the following was recorded with reference to Jack's crew in the squadron diary: 'Very quiet trip except for one fighter attack, enemy claimed as damaged.' Then there was a minelaying raid on 26/27 July off Heligoland, the squadron diary recording against Jack's crew: 'Severe electrical storms and St Elmo's fire along fuselage, wings, and propellers.' At the end of July and into August the intensity of operations continued; the enemy Navy

**Left** Flight Lieutenant Dee's, Jack's pilot's, bombing picture taken on the 4 August raid to Pauillac. *(via Anders Lund)*

```
Combat Report
No. 166 Squadron                                    Night 16/17th August 1944
Lancaster III K2 PD 153                             Fishpond Serviceable. Operator trained
03.00½ 11,000, 236T, 55.46½N. 07.25E               Homeward. Off track. 3-4 miles port of track
No cloud. No moon. Vis. starlight. Very dark        No flak, flares or other activity
Rear gunner Sgt. Fitzgerald. J. E.
150-200 rounds. 150 yards 50 yards
4 stoppages (link and ammo. stoppages)


Soon after laying mines in the Stettin area Lancaster K2 of 166 Squadron received a
warning on Fishpond of an A/C approaching fairly rapidly from slightly below almost dead
astern. About 2-3 second later the R/G obtained a visual on a Ju88 boring in from fine
port quarter at a range of approx. 150 yards. The R/G immediately opened fire at the
same time ordering a corkscrew port and observed smoke and flame pouring from both
engines of the E/A. Firing another burst the R/G then observed E/A break away on fire
about 50 yards away in the direction of the starboard beam. The M/U gunner was never
able to get in a burst due to his G.F.I. coming into operation but confirms that the
Ju88 went down in an almost vertical dive well alight. The E/A never opened fire at
any time during the attack.


Comment by S/Ldr. Cox G.G.L.
Suggested that the claim of 'Probably destroyed' be made rather than 'destroyed', as the
E/A was not seen to hit the sea and explode.
```

at Le Havre (31 July and 2 August), the V1 launch site at Le Belle Croix les Bruyeres (1 August), although poor weather hindered the attack, and the oil storage depot at Pauillac (4 and 5 August). On the latter daylight raid, there was particular tragedy for No. 166 Squadron. The squadron diary recorded:

No enemy opposition was encountered, but the operation was marred by a collision between J2 and V, whilst flying at 450ft. over the sea. As a result the tail unit and rear turret of J2 were broken off and fell into the sea. The aircraft then turned on its back and plunged into the sea and it is feared that the impact caused the bombs to detonate. The aircraft disappeared from view immediately and no survivors were seen. The mainplane of 'V' was very badly damaged and the aircraft had to abandon the mission and return to base. The remaining 21 aircraft successfully bombed the primary target but had to land away from base owing to unfavourable weather conditions.

Indeed there were no survivors from Flight Lieutenant Holman's crew, and, with no known grave, their names are now etched on the Air Forces Memorial at Runnymede.

Jack's crew must have been given leave prior to a minelaying operation on the night of 16/17 August to Stettin Bay. Jack's combat report records the action that night. (The combat report mentions 'Fishpond', an airborne radar device to give early warning of approaching German nightfighters.)

Jack's next letter home, written the day after this combat, reflects the intensity of the operations he had recently been experiencing.

Aug 17/44

My Dearest Mother & Sister
Hello Mom & Ruth I am sorry I haven't written before but it has been absolutely impossible to write we have been operating steadily with no time in between flights except to sleep. We are on now but there is a time between take off so I can dash off this letter.

I believe the last time I wrote my total of ops. was 9 well it has jumped up to 22 now and if every thing goes okay we ought to be finished pretty soon. So far we have been attacked by fighters twice and both those guys will never fly again. Last night I went on a trip and was attacked by a J.U.88 I opened up and set the guy on fire and watched him go down in flames and hit the sea and explode.

We have been doing a few battle front trips and it was really a pleasure to do them. I was talking to a Canadian officer in the army and he was telling me it was worth going over there just to see all the kites going over and knocking the living daylights out of Jerry.

What is the idea of saying I was in a Halifax bomber. Now that is an insult to us 'Lancaster!' boys and there is a sore point between the Hally & Lanc squadrons. So don't make the mistake again cause we are in aeroplanes and not flying Jalopies (Hallies).

With All my Love

Jack

After a raid to Reime on 18 August, it was a week before the crew were next operational. The night of 25/26 August 1944 is notable in that Bomber Command aircrew set a new record, flying 1,311 sorties, attacking Rüsselheim, Darmstadt, Brest and various smaller operations; diversions, minelaying, Resistance support, small Mosquito raids and patrols, and radio counter measure flights. Losses totalled twenty-five aircraft, with eight more aircraft

---

**Combat Report**

No. 166 Squadron

Lancaster III N2 LM 694

0113½ 18,000 Ft, 230T, 5000½N. 0737E

No cloud. No moon. Starlight.

Rear gunner Sgt. Fitzgerald, M/U Sgt Schafer.

Night 25/26th August 1944

Fishpond Serviceable. Operator trained Homeward on track.

Coned few mins prior to attack. No flak indiscriminate flares

Soon after leaving the target area after bombing Rüsselheim the M/U of Lanc N2 of 166 Squadron saw tracer fire from astern and slightly above. Searching the source of the trace he saw a twin engined A/C which he was unable to identify diving down from slightly above. Before he was able to bring his guns to bear in the E/A it suddenly burst into flames and dived steeply out of control. No tracer fire was observed entering the E/A from any direction. No damage was sustained by the Lancaster.

---

**Combat Report**

No. 166 Squadron

Lancaster III N2 LM 694

4.00.48 18000 Ft, 327T, 4923N. 0357E

No cloud. No moon. Starlight.

Rear gunner Sgt. Fitzgerald, 40 Rds.

Sgt Schafer.J. 50 Rds

Night 25/26th August 1944

Fishpond Serviceable. Operator trained Target on track.

Distant S/Ls. No flak

Just prior to making their bombing run the M/U of Lanc N2 of 166 Squadron observed tracer fire coming from the Port Quarter Up. He immediately identified a Ju88 at about 250 yds diving down to the attack from an angle of about 20/30 degrees. Ordering a corkscrew Port the M/U opened fire at 175 yds and was joined by the R/G who had also sighted the E/A. The E/A immediately broke away down and was not seen again. Strikes were observed by both gunners and the E/A is claimed as damaged. Two mins prior to this attack the Lanc had been attacked by an ME 109.

Comment by S/Ldr. Cox G.G.L.

The fighter was allowed to approach to within 250 yds range without being sighted; in fact the first indication of an attack was fire from the Hun. The gunners' search would appear to be not of the best. I consider that the claim of damaging the E/A is not justified.

written off in crashes on return to England. Once more John Fitzgerald was in the thick of the fighting.

There was still little rest for Jack and his crew, detailed for operations the very next night – another large-scale operational night for Bomber Command. From the 844 sorties carried out, 28 aircraft were lost. Jack Fitzgerald was to fly on a minelaying operation to the Bay of Danzig. Flight Lieutenant Dee, flying Lancaster Mk III LM694 AS-M2, lifted his four-engine bomber from the runway at RAF Kirmington at 2045 hours.

## Lancaster Mk III LM694 AS-M2 took off from RAF Kirmington at 2045 hours.

Pilot – Flight Lieutenant Fred Dee
Flight engineer – Sergeant Jack White
Navigator – Flying Officer James Russell, RCAF
Air bomber – Flying Officer George Palmer
Wireless operator – Sergeant William Holt
Mid-upper gunner – Sergeant Jacob Schafer
Rear gunner – Sergeant John Fitzgerald, DFM, RCAF

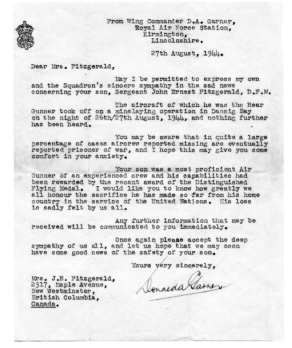

From Wing Commander D.A. Garner,
Royal Air Force Station,
Kirmington,
Lincolnshire.

27th August, 1944.

Dear Mrs. Fitzgerald,

May I be permitted to express my own and the Squadron's sincere sympathy in the sad news concerning your son, Sergeant John Ernest Fitzgerald, D.F.M.

The aircraft of which he was the Rear Gunner took off on a minelaying operation in Danzig Bay on the night of 26th/27th August, 1944, and nothing further has been heard.

You may be aware that in quite a large percentage of cases aircrew reported missing are eventually reported prisoner of war, and I hope this may give you some comfort in your anxiety.

Your son was a most proficient Air Gunner of an experienced crew and his capabilities had been rewarded by the recent award of the Distinguished Flying Medal. I would like you to know how greatly we all honour the sacrifice he has made so far from his home country in the service of the United Nations. His loss is sadly felt by us all.

Any further information that may be received will be communicated to you immediately.

Once again please accept the deep sympathy of us all, and let us hope that we may soon have some good news of the safety of your son.

Yours very sincerely,

Mrs. J.E. Fitzgerald,
2317, Maple Avenue,
New Westminster,
British Columbia,
Canada.

MINISTER OF NATIONAL DEFENCE FOR AIR

Mrs. E.V. Fitzgerald,                                        OTTAWA
2317 Maple Avenue,                                    October 4, 1944
New Westminster, British Columbia.

Dear Mrs. Fitzgerald:

At this time of great anxiety it is felt that you and the members of your family will wish to know the circumstances surrounding the honour and distinction which have come to your son Flight Sergeant John Ernest Fitzgerald DFM, through the award of the Distinguished Flying Medal for great gallantry in the performance of his duty while serving with No. 166 Squadron of the Royal Air Force.

The citation on which this award was made reads as follows:

"This airman has participated in many sorties as rear gunner. He has displayed the greatest keenness and has proved himself to be a most dependable member of aircraft crew. One night in August, 1944, Flight Sergeant Fitzgerald participated in a mine-laying mission. Shortly after leaving the target area this gunner sighted a Junkers 88. He opened fire and his first burst struck the enemy aircraft which went into a steep dive with both engines on fire. On more than one occasion his vigilance and good shooting have contributed materially to the safe return of his aircraft."

The personnel of the Force are proud of your son's fine Service record.

With kindest personal regards

Yours sincerely,

Minister of National Defence for Air

Against the names of the crew, the squadron diary later recorded: 'Failed to return. Nothing heard after take-off.' In fact 186 airmen failed to return from operations that night. Some 186 'regret to' telegrams were dispatched to next of kin.

FORM 6122

| CLASS OF SERVICE | SYMBOL |
|---|---|
| Full-Rate Message | |
| Day Letter | D L |
| Night Message | N M |
| Night Letter | N L |

If none of these three symbols appears after the check (number of words) this is a full-rate message. Otherwise its character is indicated by the symbol appearing after the check.

# CANADIAN NATIONAL TELEGRAM

W. M. ARMSTRONG, GENERAL MANAGER, TORONTO, ONT,

Exclusive Connection with
WESTERN UNION CABLES
Cable Service to all the World
Money Transferred by Telegraph

STANDARD TIME    1944 AUG 30 PM 9 34

RXVA74 33 2 EXTRA BC= RCAF OTTAWA ONT 30 1137P=

MRS J E FITZGERALD REPORT DELIVERY=

2317 MAPLE AVE NEWWESTMINSTER BC=

M9854 REGRET TO ADVISE THAT YOUR SON R TWO ONE FIVE TWO ONE

NOUGHT SERGEANT JOHN ERNEST FITZGERALD IS REPORTED MISSING

AFTER AIR OPERATIONS OVERSEAS AUGUST TWENTY SEVENTH STOP

LETTER FOLLOWS= RCAF CAUSALTIES OFFICER.

**Left** The awful news.

---

ADDRESS REPLY TO:
THE SECRETARY,
DEPARTMENT OF NATIONAL DEFENCE FOR AIR,
OTTAWA, ONTARIO.

OUR FILE  R215210 (R.O.4)
REF. YOUR
DATED

## ROYAL CANADIAN AIR FORCE

OTTAWA, Canada, 30th November, 1944.

Mrs. J.E. Fitzgerald,
2317 Maple Avenue,
New Westminster, B.C.

Dear Mrs. Fitzgerald:

I must regretfully inform you that since your son, Sergeant John Ernest Fitzgerald, was reported missing no further information regarding him has been received other than that contained in the letter to you dated September 5th from these Headquarters.

You may rest assure that every possible effort is being made to trace your son and upon any news being obtained you will be informed immediately.

May I extend my sincere sympathy to you and the members of your family in this time of anxiety.

Yours sincerely,

R.C.A.F. Casualty Officer,
for Chief of the Air Staff.

R.C.A.F. G. 79D

---

ADDRESS REPLY TO:
THE SECRETARY,
DEPARTMENT OF NATIONAL DEFENCE FOR AIR,
OTTAWA, ONTARIO.

OUR FILE  R215210 (R.O.4)
REF. YOUR
DATED

## ROYAL CANADIAN AIR FORCE

OTTAWA, Canada, 27th June, 1946.

Mrs. J.E. Fitzgerald,
2317 Maple Avenue,
New Westminster, B.C.

Dear Mrs. Fitzgerald:

A report has been received from the Royal Air Force Missing Research and Enquiry Service on the Continent giving the results of their investigations concerning the fate of your son, Flight Sergeant John Ernest Fitzgerald, D.F.M., and his crew.

The report states that at 3:30 A.M. on the morning of August 27th, 1944, the aircraft in which your son was flying was observed amongst a number of others in combat at a low altitude and was seen to crash over the estate of Mr. Svend Anderson at Traeden, Denmark. The local inhabitants were prevented from approaching the scene of the accident but saw the Germans recover the bodies of the crew which they transported to Gamle Rye Cemetery.

Due to the severe nature of the crash, however, Pilot Officer White was the only member of the crew who could be identified and the entire crew were interred in a communal grave and it is numbered Row 9, Plot 11, Grave # 14, a photograph of which is enclosed.

The reverent care of the burial places of all who served in the Forces of the British Empire is the task of the Imperial War Graves Commission. Already eminent architects are at work, planning the construction of beautiful cemeteries and each individual grave will be supported and sustained by the nations of the Empire. I hope that it may be of some consolation to you to know that your gallant son's grave is in sacred care and keeping.

May I again extend my most sincere sympathy.

Yours sincerely,

R.C.A.F. Casualty Officer,
for Chief of the Air Staff.

R.C.A.F. G. 32B

**Far left** Missing letter to Jack's mother 30 November 1944.

**Left** Post-war letter to Jack's mother confirming the fate of her son.

*(The No. 166 Squadron Lancaster of Flying Officer R. G. Bradley, RCAF, was also lost on the night of 26/27 August 1944, coming down into the sea with a total loss of life. Only the bodies of the pilot and one other member were found.)*

In the early hours of 27 August 1944 Flight Lieutenant Frederick Dee's burning Lancaster smashed into the ground near the village of Åstruplund and exploded. Some local people, initially transfixed as the fireball passed overhead, rushed to the crash site. One man recovered a parachute; his wife would appreciate the silk. Later that morning, with the area cordoned off, Svend Andersen, the owner of the field, approached, concerned about his crops. With permission granted, Svend neared the scene of devastation. He would never recover from what he then witnessed. Scorched pieces of wreckage and the horror of charred human remains were strewn across his field. Svend's nose filled with the acrid fumes of burning wheel rubber mixed with the distasteful stench of burnt flesh. With ammunition occasionally exploding, German soldiers gathered up body parts using whatever tools they had at hand, secreting them in paper bags. As the day went on more locals would regret making a visit to the scene of the crash.

That evening the body bags were taken away. Three days later, on the morning of 30 August, German soldiers sealed off all access to the churchyard at the town of GL. Rye. Here the entire crew were buried, without dignity. The gravedigger and another local man had quietly gained access to the church tower and they later told how, with no vicar present, the soldiers kicked the bags into the graves. A few days later the Germans erected a white wooden cross.

For two weeks the Germans maintained a cordon around the crash site. Much of what remained of the Lancaster was recovered, anything of use to be sent back to Germany. Outside the cordon Svend had noticed a piece of the spar, and his farm hand, Rasmus Due Andersen, surreptitiously placed it at the bottom of a cart, covering it with

**Right** GL. Rye Churchyard, Denmark, and the collective grave of the crew of Flight Lieutenant Dee.

After the war, on 5 February 1946, Svend received a visit from a Captain Adams and two RAF officers, informing them of the details of the crash. It was now possible to expand upon the 'reported missing' information that relatives of the seven airmen had previously had.

Shortly after this visit Svend found out that a local person had the dog tag of one of the airmen, Jack White. This was sent to his mother, and she passed on information about the names of the other airmen lost that night and addresses of relatives. The memorial cross was engraved accordingly, photographed and copies sent to the relatives. Over the years Svend maintained contact with the relatives, many of whom paid him a visit. In June 1976 Jack White's mother and sister came to Denmark. Svend's grandson Anders Lund remembers it well.

A visit that made a great impression on me was when Mrs White and her daughter, the mother and the sister of Jack White, visited my grandparents. The mother, Mrs White was 82 years old, and her last wish was to see her son's grave. For 30 years, she had, in letters to my grandfather, expressed a wish to see the last resting place of her son. It was very emotional to see Mrs White pause by her son's grave. The visit had a strong effect on both my grandfather and Mrs White and her daughter. At the request of the Whites, my grandfather received a Royal Air Force coat of arms in appreciation for his work with the memorial cross. Today this coat of arms, received by him in 1976, is hanging in my home, in my best room.

My grandfather was not a member of the Resistance or in any way active in the war. His war effort was to contact the surviving relatives of the crew. As he would say, 'We, having been most closely involved, will never forget it. They spent their lives so that we could live in a free country.' ●

animal feed. A German soldier followed Rasmus home, the Dane unsure if he had been seen, but shortly before entering the farmyard the soldier went his separate way. The spar was stashed away in a loft, and after the war Svend tasked a local blacksmith with turning it into a memorial cross.

**Left** Memorial cross commemorating the crash of Lancaster LM694 on the night of 26/27 August 1944. *(Anders Lund)*

**Left inset** In 1976 Jack White's mother and sister visit his grave, buried with the rest of his crew. Beneath Jack Fitzgerald's name was 'Love and Remembrance Last For Ever'. *(Anders Lund)*

## CHAPTER TEN

# LOST OVER HANOVER

## STEVE BOND

THROUGHOUT THE LAST FEW MONTHS OF THE SECOND WORLD WAR, THE BOMBER COMMAND CAMPAIGN CONTINUED UNABATED. ALTHOUGH THE LUFTWAFFE'S EFFECTIVENESS DECLINED SHARPLY THROUGH LACK OF BOTH EXPERIENCED CREWS AND FUEL, ALLIED DAY AND NIGHT RAIDS OVER ENEMY-HELD TERRITORY REMAINED HIGHLY RISKY FOR THE BOMBER CREWS – RIGHT TO THE END. MEN CONTINUED TO BE LOST, AND VETERAN JACK BROMFIELD VIVIDLY RECALLS THE SIGNS BACK AT BASE THAT HIGHLIGHTED SOMEONE HAD FAILED TO RETURN. 'WHAT USED TO GET ME WAS BREAKFAST THE NEXT MORNING. YOU'D EXPECT TO SEE SEVEN BLOKES SITTING AT A TABLE AND THEY WEREN'T THERE. THEN YOU SAT AROUND FOR A WHILE, WONDERING IF THEY HAD LANDED AWAY FROM HOME. BY DINNER TIME YOU KNEW. THESE MEMORIES ARE STILL THERE. THEY'RE THERE ALL THE TIME. YOU CAN GO, MAYBE, TWO WEEKS AND THINK NOTHING; THERE'S A LITTLE SNIPPET IN THE PAPER OR ON THE TELEVISION AND SUDDENLY IT ALL STARTS TO WIND UP AGAIN. OR SOMEBODY MENTIONS A NAME, YOU'VE FORGOTTEN ABOUT HIM FOR YEARS, AND SUDDENLY YOU REMEMBER.'

O N  T H E  N I G H T  of 5/6 January 1945 Bomber Command launched its first large-scale raid on Hanover since October 1943, with a force of 664 aircraft, of which 23 Handley Page Halifaxes and 8 Avro Lancasters were lost; one of these was Halifax III MZ432/NP-Q of No. 158 Squadron based at RAF Lissett in Yorkshire. The crew comprised skipper Flying Officer Arthur 'Robbie' Robertson, Royal Canadian Air Force (RCAF) from Branton, Manitoba, navigator Flight Sergeant Tom 'Jock' Laurie, RAF, from Auchinleck, Ayrshire, bomb aimer Flying Officer Gar Cross, RCAF, from Vancouver, wireless operator Flight Sergeant Jack Bromfield, RAF, from Bletchley, Buckinghamshire, flight engineer Sergeant George Dacey, RAF, from Liverpool, mid-upper gunner Warrant Officer Gerry Marion, RCAF, from Lethbridge, Alberta, and rear gunner Flight Sergeant Ed Rae, RCAF, from Ottawa.

This was the crew's twelfth operation, their first having been a daylight raid on 16 November 1944 to attack German troop concentrations at Julik. As Jack Bromfield recalls: 'That frightened the bloody life out of me! I've never seen so much flak in all my life. But we gelled as a crew, except with the flight engineer, who always seemed to be on the outside looking in. Then we went to Mannheim, Cologne, Koblenz, Sterkrade, when we went after the oil refineries, you know, the usual run-of-the-mill targets.'

On the fateful night, they were flying with a replacement flight engineer who was joining them for the first time. The regular flight engineer was from London and, as Jack says: 'He didn't go that night, he'd disappeared, and we don't know where he went, or what happened to him. When I asked the skipper where he was, he just said "He isn't coming." After I eventually got back to England in the summer of 1945, I bumped into him at Cosford, but only got "Hello, goodbye", as quick as that.' For all seven men aboard 'Queenie', the take-off at just

**Left** No. 6 Group Battle School, Dalton, Yorkshire – escape and evasion training. Left to right: Tom Laurie, Ed Rae, Gar Cross, Jack Bromfield, Robbie Robertson, Gerry Marion. *(Jack Bromfield)*

after 5 p.m. would be the last time they would see RAF Lissett.

Just over two hours later, as the bomber stream was approaching Hanover from the north-west, Robertson's Halifax was attacked by a nightfighter, which the rear gunner spotted and identified as a Ju.88. The fighter was flown by Hauptmann Heinz Rökker, Knight's Cross with Oak Leaves, based with Nachtjagdgeschwader 2 at Twente in Holland, who ended the war with a total of sixty-four victories. The Halifax was hit twice, with each attack following the usual approach from below the bomber so that the Schräge Musik upward-firing cannons could be used, so the rear gunner was lucky to have seen it at all. Jack continues: 'There was a hell of a lot of bangs and thumps and crashes, and then a fire started in the bomb bay.'

There were bits flying off here, there and everywhere. I didn't know until some days afterwards that I'd been shot on the outside of the foot, but my feet were so bloody cold I didn't feel it. Anyhow, things went from bad to worse, but the aircraft didn't do anything strange, it was just losing height. I looked past my curtain at the pilot, and he looked at me and pulled the control column backwards and forwards and said 'I've got no control', so he said 'Right, time to go.' It was only a shallow dive, the aircraft was still quite steady on its feet, it wasn't rolling or whatever. But there was no point in staying with it if we put the fire out, because it just wouldn't come out of the dive. So out we went.

After a considerable struggle with the latching mechanism, Jack was eventually able to open the hatch between himself and the navigator, which was where the navigator, bomb aimer and wireless operator would go out. The wireless operator also had the job of giving the pilot his parachute, because it was stowed next to his on the starboard side, and the pilot would then follow the other three out. The mid-upper gunner and the flight engineer would go out of the rear door, while the rear gunner, who had a fighter-type parachute, just turned his turret to one side and rolled out backwards. However, at the time the crew thought that George Dacey, the flight engineer, and at 35 the old man of the crew, had not got out. The last Jack saw of him he was standing in mid-fuselage, and he did not subsequently turn up with the rest of the crew in captivity.

Having successfully abandoned the aircraft, Jack remembers hearing the sound of the Jumo engines of a nightfighter, perhaps the one that had shot them down. He then had to think about his landing. 'I went through two lots of cloud and then it was white, just a white-out on the ground.'

I could see the target burning, and I could see flares going down, so I knew we weren't far, but the bombs were still on when we left her; we hadn't bombed. Anyway, I couldn't steer this bloody thing, so I thought well, training, turn the buckle and hit it. I did, and I fell out of the harness, straight on my arse in the middle of the road. It was a very wooded area, so I buried my 'chute and harness, and having seen the direction of the target, I knew which was south east and which was west, so I just buggered off in a westerly direction, thinking I might bump into somebody, but I didn't see a soul. I didn't see another 'chute, I didn't see anything at all. I had

**Left** No. 158 Squadron RAF Lissett, 1944. Left to right: Jack Bromfield, Gerry Marion, Gar Cross, Tom Laurie. *(Jack Bromfield)*

eight days on the run, and I thought I was doing quite well, hiding up in the day and walked at night. But I gave that up after two days because I got fed up of tripping over tree roots and falling down ruddy ditches in the dark. About the third or fourth morning, I was walking just off a road in the woods, and I heard voices; I could understand what they were saying. I thought 'Some other members of the crew', but I'll be cagey, just in case it isn't. I got towards the edge of the wood and looked down the road, and there's two blokes with shotguns and three blokes standing with their hands up. They were Americans, you could tell by their flying boots; they were funny little things they used to have compared to ours. So, discretion being the better part of valour, I went deeper into the woods and just kept on walking and never saw anything of them again.

**Left** No. 21 OTU, RAF Moreton-in-Marsh, Robbie Robertson. *(Jack Bromfield)*

On the eighth day, Jack was following a single-track railway line going west, and by now he was getting very hungry. He saw a field that looked promising as a possible source of food and started scratching about in the soil to get what looked like swedes, which would have been better than nothing. Suddenly he felt something in the middle of his back, and a voice said 'Hande hock!' He did and when he turned round there was a man in a railway uniform who had seen him from a small station hidden behind the trees. Soon after that two Luftwaffe men came along in what Jack describes as a clapped-out Beetle and took him away.

Mid-upper gunner Gerry Marion had also successfully abandoned the doomed Halifax, leaving by the rear door. He too parachuted onto a road, but was almost immediately captured, wounded

**Right** No. 21 OTU,
RAF Moreton-in-
Marsh. Top to
bottom, Robbie
Robertson, Gar Cross,
Tom Laurie, Gerry
Marion, Jack
Bromfield, Ed Rae.
(*Jack Bromfield*)

with a broken leg caused by gunshot, roughed up and taken to a guardhouse. The next morning he was taken by car, with two guards, on a two-hour drive to another guardhouse. There he spent two weeks in solitary, the only POW there, with no one to talk to. He left on 19 January with a German officer, and met another guard and a burnt American flyer and guard at Kassel. They then spent two days on a train to Frankfurt, with lots of problems, arriving on 20 January. Gerry continues:

We then went to the air force interrogation centre (sweat-box) at Dulag Luft. Later that month I went to Hohemark Hospital by truck, for medical treatment; my leg was in bad shape. There were 15 to 20 other POWs there. Then, still in January, I had to endure a forced march and boxcar ride with 15 POWs and five guards to Nürnberg POW camp, Stalag XIIIC, with approximately 2,000 POWs. Then in February, the camp was evacuated and we were marched to another camp at Moosburg, Stalag VIIA. At both Nürnberg and Moosburg we slept in tents.

The remaining crew members were also rounded up by the Germans very quickly and spent the rest of the war in captivity. However, nothing was ever seen of George Dacey, and for many years the survivors believed that he had simply failed to get out of the burning Halifax. Certainly no body was ever found, and Dacey is commemorated on Panel 274 at the Air Forces Memorial at Runnymede.

Many years after the war, it was Gerry Marion (who had been held in a different POW camp from the rest) who finally contacted other members of the crew with some information concerning George's

**Right and below**
In July 2004 at the Oldenburg home of Hauptmann Heinz Rökker (Knight's Cross with Oakleaves and the seventh highest scoring Luftwaffe nightfighter ace, 64 victories with NJG2) Jack Bromfield meets the man who shot his Halifax down. Author Steve Bond was with Jack, '...they got on like a house on fire...'. *(Steve Bond)*

fate. Sometime after his capture, Gerry had met an American airman who had been injured and taken to a German hospital. There he met George Dacey, who had been quite badly injured when he bailed out. It seems that George decided that, if he was going to escape, doing so from a hospital was likely to be far easier than from a POW camp. When he attempted to do so, he was shot, and more than likely he was hurriedly buried in the vicinity.

The surviving crew were finally liberated – five, including Jack, from Stalag Luft 1 at Barth in northern Germany on the Baltic coast.

One night we heard these bangs, and thumps, and somebody said 'That's the Russian guns.' When we got up next morning, there were Russians in the compound and there was a lot of conversation going on outside between the commissioned types in the camp and the Russians, and then they cleared off and just left us to our own devices. Then suddenly this hoard of B-17s appeared and landed, and that's what I flew home in, landing at Ford down near Littlehampton.

Gerry Marion had been held in Stalag VIIA at Moosburg in southern Germany, which was the largest of all the German POW camps; at the time of its liberation there were around 40,000 men in a camp designed to hold 10,000: 'We were released in April by American Army General Patton. I was flown to Reims, France, then to army hospital in England. There was nothing first class on this trip.'

Following their release and demobilization, the surviving members of the crew returned to their home towns. Sadly, Robbie Robertson was killed in the late 1940s in a flying accident in Canada while flying a North American B-25 Mitchell. ●

## CHAPTER ELEVEN

# 'A PRIVILEGE TO SERVE'

## STEVE DARLOW

FLIGHT LIEUTENANT DESMOND PELLY, DFC, CONSIDERS IT A PRIVILEGE TO HAVE SERVED WITH THE ROYAL AIR FORCE AND BOMBER COMMAND DURING THE SECOND WORLD WAR. DESMOND'S EARLY OPERATIONAL EXPERIENCE WAS GAINED FLYING WITH THE MAIN FORCE, BUT HIS, AND HIS CREW'S TALENTS FOR THE TASK AT HAND, LED TO SELECTION FOR PATH FINDER DUTIES – TO ILLUMINATE AND IDENTIFY TARGETS, TO MARK AIMING POINTS AND TO LEAD RAIDS. DESMOND'S CREW CONTINUALLY PROVED THEIR ABILITY, PASSING THE TWENTY OPERATION MARK, THEN THIRTY, THEN FORTY, AND THEIR RESPONSIBILITIES GREW, AMID THE EVER-PRESENT DANGER OF FLYING IN HOSTILE SKIES. DESPITE SKILL AND EXPERIENCE, THEY ULTIMATELY FELL FOUL OF THE PROBABILITIES STACKED AGAINST BOMBER CREWS, SUCCUMBING TO THE GERMAN DEFENCES ON THE NIGHT OF 20/21 FEBRUARY 1945. DESMOND'S LANCASTER WAS RAKED WITH CANNON SHELL, THE FUEL TANKS BURST INTO FLAME AND HE FOUND HIMSELF FIGHTING TO HOLD THE FLAMING LANCASTER STEADY SO THAT HIS CREW COULD ESCAPE WITH THEIR LIVES.

ANDREW DESMOND PELLY joined the air force on his 18th birthday and was called up in February 1942. Born on 28 August 1923, in Godstone, Surrey, Desmond was educated at Charterhouse, became a member of the Air Training Corps, and through his teenage years developed an interest in 'speed in general'.

Upon call-up for aircrew duties, Desmond journeyed through the typical training process; he was kitted out at Lord's cricket ground, underwent square bashing in Scarborough and was then sent

School near Exeter, Ontario, flying Avro Ansons. 'It had been decided at Goderich whether you went on single engine or multi-engine. I was never interested in aerobatics and that sort of thing so I was definitely for multi-engine aircraft.' At the end of April 1943, and having received his Wings, Desmond, frustratingly, was sent on an instructors' course. 'This was not for me at all. I was only 20 and I didn't want to spend the rest of the war instructing out in Canada. So I managed to fail my instructor's course by not having a voice loud

**Left** Desmond Pelly's 'Above the Average' assessment following training as a bomber pilot, 17 May 1944. *(Desmond Pelly)*

to Carlisle to start flying in De Havilland Tiger Moths. After awaiting an overseas posting at Heaton Park in Manchester, Desmond travelled on the *Queen Elizabeth* from Glasgow to New York, then on to a holding camp at Moncton, Canada, and finally to Goderich, Ontario and No. 12 Elementary Flying Training School, still on Tiger Moths, arriving in October 1942. Subsequently came a posting to No. 9 Service Flying Training

enough for instructing.' In June 1943 Desmond made his way back to the UK on the *Queen Elizabeth*. Then there was more frustration, with further tests – 'They wanted to find out how our training had gone in Canada' – and a posting to No. 18 Advanced Flying Unit at RAF Snitterfield, flying Airspeed Oxfords and familiarizing himself with black-out and wartime conditions. A Beam Approach course followed at RAF Coningsby and then a return to RAF Snitterfield. The delay was getting to Desmond; typical of aircrew in similar situations, he wanted to put into practice his newfound skills: 'Having done all that training, there was no place for me in Bomber Command.'

Matters were not about to improve. From December 1943 to March 1944 Desmond acted as a second pilot with the Air Transport Auxiliary. Although he appreciated the experience of flying various types of aircraft in bad weather conditions, he was anxious to move on: 'It was interesting but very frustrating. I wanted to get on to operations!'

exposed to flying in hostile air space. The level of danger had risen and for some it proved too much. 'Six of us took off and only three of us got back. One was shot down over France. One had engine trouble and landed somewhere in the south of England, and one crashed back at base.' Even though they were still at a training unit, the perils of flying were clear. 'There were one or two accidents. We personally were lucky, we didn't. I do remember one Wellington crashing and killing the whole crew. You shrugged it off and said "Oh well let's hope it doesn't happen to us."'

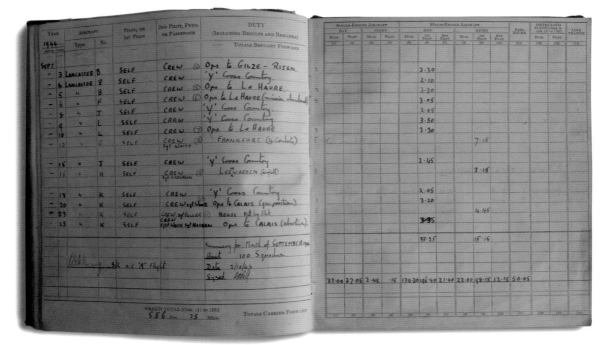

**Right** Desmond Pelly's September 1944 operations with No. 100 Squadron, detailed in his logbook, including mention of the 'four combats' on the 12 September raid to Frankfurt. *(Desmond Pelly)*

Finally his chance came with a posting to No. 30 Operational Training Unit to fly Vickers Wellingtons and begin the crewing-up process. Airmen from the various aircrew trades 'were all put together and a chap came up to me who had been on the same pilot's course as I had in Canada. He had failed and then trained as a navigator. "I'd like to be your navigator," he said. "Fine," I replied. Then we sort of wandered around and somehow got ourselves together.'

While at OTU Desmond took his crew on a 'Nickel' (leaflet dropping) raid to Châteaudun. Such raids were seen as relatively 'easy' operations and a means by which new crews were initially

Midway through June 1944 Desmond and his crew were sent to No. 1667 Conversion Unit at RAF Sandtoft, Lincolnshire, to gain experience on four-engine aircraft, flying the Handley Page Halifax bomber. They also picked up their flight engineer. The crew began to bond, the personalities and abilities moulded into a team, and Desmond, as captain, established their modus operandi.

We were a very closely knit crew. We'd go off to the pub together, if one had a birthday we celebrated that in a big way – always socializing together, nothing like officers and other ranks. We were a crew and we were going to work together. The closer you got together, the more efficient you became.

We were very disciplined in the air. I was extremely strict. I would not allow any crew to talk other than on the business we were doing. If they had something to say about the operation, such as the navigator giving a course, or the radio operator telling me of a message, or the gunners warning about fighters, sure fine, but no back chat at all. I spoke to every member of the crew every ten minutes, to make sure they were awake and on the ball. Also making sure they had their oxygen supply, which was very important. We did have one occasion when the navigator passed out. He had pinched his oxygen tube leaning against his table – passed out completely. We pumped oxygen into him and he recovered.

On 17 July Desmond transferred with his crew to No. 1 Lancaster Finishing School at RAF Hemswell, Lincolnshire. 'The Avro Lancaster was the finest bomber that was ever made, at that stage. I was very very impressed.' Then on 10 August Desmond arrived at No. 100 Squadron at RAF Waltham, Lincolnshire. 'This was what we had trained for. We were all very pleased to get on an operational squadron.'

There was a very good friend of mine, Christopher Holland, who I knew before the war, and he and I joined the squadron on virtually the same day. We had gone through all the training more or less together. I had some leave immediately and went off for a few days and when I came back he was missing – on his very first trip. It was a bit of a shock at that stage to somebody who actually hadn't done an operation.

On 25 August Desmond took part in his first sortie to Germany, to Rüsselheim, as a second dickie (second pilot) – a familiarization with another crew: 'One was nervous, no question about it, but once in the aircraft and flying you forgot that; you were too busy doing your job. I remember approaching the target and thinking "That's dangerous, how are we going to get through all that."' Then on 29 August came the first raid with his normal crew, to Stettin on the Baltic coast, a round trip of 8 hours

55 minutes. 'Coming back I remember how very tired I was and so were the crew. I had to keep them on the ball right the way back, not to sleep.' Over the course of the next eleven days Desmond was sent on operations six times, all daylight raids. Then on 12 September he was detailed to take part in an attack on Frankfurt. That night Desmond's combat piloting skills would be tested to the full. 'My gunners said that they had shot one fighter down, but we couldn't actually claim it as we didn't see it hit the ground. They said it was going down with smoke coming out of its engine.'

**Left** Desmond Pelly's certificate acknowledging his award of the Path Finder Force Badge. *(Desmond Pelly)*

On 16 September Desmond took part in a raid to Leeuwarden airfield, followed by a daylight to Calais, still garrisoned by German forces, on the 20th, and a night raid to Neuss on the 23rd, during which the aircraft suffered flak damage. On 5 October the crew were detailed to attack Saarbrücken. 'The Squadron Commander said in briefing that he had been asked to provide a Path Finder crew and he would decide the following morning which crew.' At that stage of the war the Path Finder Force (No. 8 Group), which had been established to assist in the location and marking of targets for the main force, had been in existence for just over two years. The Path Finder Force was always on the look-out

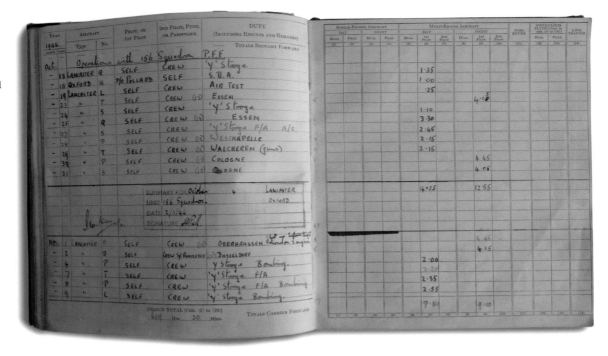

for crews that showed the potential to meet their
exacting operational duties. Desmond Pelly's crew
had shown such potential. 'We were appointed and
I was delighted. I said to my crew, "Do you want to
come to Path Finders with me? You have the option,
if you want, to stay in the main force and do your
30 operations." They all came with me.'

A short training period followed at RAF
Warboys, Huntingdonshire. Desmond's original
bomb aimer became the 'H2S' (ground scanning
radar) operator, so a new eighth member of the
crew took up bomb-aiming duties. Midway through
October the crew arrived at No. 156 Squadron:
'A wonderful squadron, they really were. Morale
was immensely high, despite a major accident the
month before when de-bombing an aircraft – one
of the bombs exploded killing a lot of chaps.'

We had a magnificent squadron commander,
Wing Commander Ison, a key man in the morale.
He had done an awful lot of trips himself and
knew what it was all about. At this stage he was
off operations because he had done at least two
tours. He knew what we were going through.
The flight commanders were chaps who had
completed many trips and knew what it was all
about. Morale was good. I consider myself very

privileged from the point of view that Wing
Commander Ison and I got on particularly well
and I flew his aeroplane the whole time.

On 23 October Desmond's crew attacked one of
the most heavily defended targets, Essen; they were
given the task of illuminating the aiming point.
Then over the next few months, as they gained
experience and proved themselves, their levels of
responsibility rose.

When we first joined the Path Finders we were
given the job of going in first and dropping flares
to light up the whole target. Then having dropped
the flares we went round for about 10 minutes and
then round again to drop the bombs, by which
time the Master Bomber was in place and the first
T.I. [Target Indicators – coloured pyrotechnics]
had gone down. You dropped your bombs on the
T.I. or on whatever the Master Bomber instructed.

Then we were promoted to taking T.I., as back-
up markers. The primary markers would go in
after the target had been lit up. Then every two
or three minutes back-up markers would come in
– the initial markers would have been obliterated
by bombs. All through the raid back-up would be
coming in. So from lighting up a target you be-

came a back-up marker and then finally a primary marker. After that you were promoted to Deputy Master Bomber and finally Master Bomber.

Over the course of the next four months Desmond's logbook filled with operational details. Following his nineteenth, on 1 November, to Oberhaussen, he wrote in his logbook: 'Shot up before target. Returned on 3 engines.' On 2 January 1945 he completed his thirtieth operation, an attack on the railyards at Nürnberg. Indeed most of the raids Desmond flew on during this period were to rail targets, as Bomber Command sought to disrupt German communications behind the battle fronts, hindering enemy troop reinforcement and the movement of supplies. Then on 20 February 1945 Desmond was detailed for his fortieth operation (his forty-first including the OTU Nickel raid) to Reisholz.

*(Matters became complicated for the Bomber Command raid planners on 20 February 1945. An unpredictable weather front led to a switch of target for over 500 Lancasters, dispatched instead to the Ruhr and Dortmund (eventually 514 Lancasters and 14 Mosquitoes took off). With two other bomber forces, predominantly Halifax bombers, detailed for attacks on targets between Cologne and Düsseldorf; Reisholz (156 Halifaxes, 11 Mosquitoes, and 6 Lancasters) and*

*Monheim (112 Halifaxes, 10 Mosquitoes, and 6 Lancasters), and then one other force to attack Gravenhorst 50 miles north, somehow the raids had to be coordinated. As the post-raid Bomber Command narrative put it: 'The resultant plan of operations… was extremely complicated.' The Dortmund force was sent westwards between Cologne and Düsseldorf, at the same time as the Gravenhorst force. Then the Reisholz and Monheim forces, sent beyond to the east of the Ruhr, were brought in westwards through the gap vacated by the Dortmund and Gravenhorst attackers. 'Thus nearly 800 bombers were operating in a fairly small area, sufficient time being allowed to prevent a head-on clash between the Lancasters and Halifaxes north of Cologne. This plan, though far from ideal, was the only practicable scheme in the circumstances.' Desmond Pelly, in his Lancaster, was carrying out his Path Finder duties at the forefront of the Reisholz Halifax force.*

*Various other smaller raids were carried out as diversionary measures, to keep the German nightfighter controllers guessing, and Bomber Command analysts would later give them some credit; however, nightfighters based in the Ruhr area did manage to penetrate the Dortmund stream as it passed through the gap between Düsseldorf and Cologne and in the run-up to the target area. There was intense combat as the bomber aircrews fought for their lives. Ultimately fourteen Lancasters failed to return from the raid; most were lost in aerial combat with the enemy. With the Luftwaffe's nightfighters now in the air, many then found fresh contacts in the*

**Left** As 1944 drew to a close, and as the Allied armies advanced to the German border, Bomber Command carried out a sustained campaign against German transportation targets including the rail network. Through December 1944 Desmond Pelly played his part. *(Desmond Pelly)*

Map © Fighting High
*(Steve Darlow)*

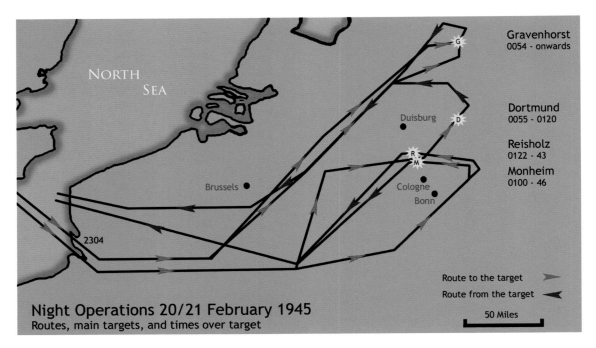

Gravenhorst
0054 - onwards

Dortmund
0055 - 0120

Reisholz
0122 - 43

Monheim
0100 - 46

Route to the target
Route from the target

**Night Operations 20/21 February 1945**
Routes, main targets, and times over target

50 Miles

*Cologne area as the Reisholz and Monheim forces, heading east, approached their targets. Four Halifaxes and one Lancaster failed to return from the Reisholz raid and two Halifaxes were lost on the Monheim attack. As Desmond Pelly was approaching his designated target, the nightfighters were waiting.*

There were two Path Finders, myself and one other. I was Deputy Master Bomber. Everything had gone perfectly smoothly until we were approaching the target and I realized there was a certain amount of fighter activity. I saw one, if not two other aircraft shot down. We actually had our bomb doors open and I was under the direction of the bomb aimer. We only had about fifteen seconds or so to go before we had to drop our bombs. I saw a German fighter and warned the gunners: 'There's a fighter right underneath us now.' The words were hardly out of my mouth and up came the cannon shells, right across all our petrol tanks. Immediately I could see there was no way I was going to get the fire out of the petrol tanks and I gave the orders to abandon the aircraft; the fires were right across the tanks. Fortunately the fighter had not hit any of our bombs. I think that was on purpose – if he had hit one of the bombs it might have blown him out of the sky as well as us.

I kept the aircraft flying. The bomb aimer was right down in the nose, I knew he would have got out. I saw my two navigators go past me and my engineer had gone. They'd had enough time to get out so I reckoned the radio operator and two gunners would have had time to get out of the back. On the other hand I was pretty certain at that stage that the rear gunner had been killed. The aircraft was very badly damaged. My navigator went out and for some reason his parachute didn't open. The mid-upper gunner panicked before he got out and opened his parachute in the aircraft. He jumped with it and it got caught on the tail plane and he went down with the aircraft.

When I was satisfied all who survived had got out I dived out of the forward hatch. The last I saw of the altimeter we were down to around 10,000 feet. The aircraft was going down pretty quickly. I hadn't got much control and it was going down in a bit of a spiral. Eventually the parachute opened and I floated peacefully down, landing in a German field. My radio operator, who got out before me, told me afterwards that he saw the aircraft blow up shortly after we had got out.

Desmond had survived, along with four other members of his crew. Navigator Flying Officer David Sinfield, DFC, and air gunners Flight

Sergeant Eric Bangs and Flight Sergeant Thomas Carr did not survive the nightfighter attack, and were ultimately laid to rest in Rheinberg War Cemetery.

Desmond's following experiences can be based on a 'diary'. Without writing paper Desmond recorded events on the back of cigarette packets, starting the night he was shot down. In recent times Desmond has been able to expand on some of the incidents.

**Notes made by A. D. P. on back of cigarette packets during his time in Germany, 21/2/45– 4/5/45**

**Two crews briefed for raid. Take off 10.40. Bright, moonlit night. All normal until running in on target (Reisholz) hit by cannon shells from nightfighter in starboard inner tank and elevators. Immediate fierce fire. Fire increased so told crew to bale out (at about 17,000 feet). Fear of explosion. Rear Gunner probably shot;**

**later tried to contact him on intercom but failed. Very little control of aircraft. Before leaving, aircraft out of control in spiral dive; tanks blow up. Slightly burnt on left leg. Last look at altimeter 10,000.**

**Grand feeling floating down, but very fed up. Fighter circles my parachute.**

**Landed safely in open country; leave parachute and Mae West where I landed. Walk about five miles west during night. Lay up all Wednesday in wood outside village. Frozen all day. A lot of bombing by Americans rather too close (30 miles)!!**

**Start at 5 p.m. when still light. Walk into army camp, but get away unseen. Steer due west across country; several near shaves in villages and gardens. Eventually hit road to town a few miles north of Cologne. Leg begins to hurt badly, but press on till 10 p.m. Short rest, then walk through village. See big raid on Duisberg in progress. Continue towards Cologne until leg too painful to walk on, so lay in ditch outside village. Very cold and hungry, having**

**Left** No. 156 Squadron December 1944, RAF Upwood. Desmond, front row seated, second from the right.
*(Desmond Pelly)*

covered twenty miles in five hours across country. Fall asleep.

Woken up by bayonets of two army privates; try to pass off as Frenchman, but marched to guard house and identified. Slept there all night. Smuggled food and water by privates when no N.C.O or Officer was looking. Taken to Gestapo H.Q. and interrogated; would not answer anything.

It was perfectly civil. They were not unpleasant in any way. We had, the night we were shot down, some new navigational equipment on our aircraft I was completely unaware of what exactly it was. They had found that and wanted to know what it was and what it did. They did give both myself and the crew quite an interrogation. Under the Geneva Convention name, rank, and number, is all you have to give. I hope all my crew did that. I certainly did.

**Put on truck to Cologne with one miserable guard. Civilians very hostile. A flat city. Slipped food when no one was looking.**

I was taken by a single guard through Cologne in the night, and that night the RAF decided to bomb Cologne. The guard decided that he would take me to the air raid shelter under Cologne Cathedral. When we got there the inhabitants were very dangerous. They wanted to kill me, as simple as that. The guard then decided it would be best to be under the RAF bombs than down in the shelter. He took me straight out.

**Taken to drome, much safer locked up than near civilians. Interrogated by 'pretty girl', but would not respond.**

The Germans put before me the most gorgeous German girl, who offered all that she could in exchange for information. She got, I can assure you, only my name, rank and number.

**Joined Reg (engineer) and several others. Fed well – no drinking water, only allowed acorn coffee, horrible stuff – but bored stiff. Plenty of air activity towards the west.**

Guns continuous; obviously a push on.

**Stayed here till Saturday evening 24/2/45. Thirteen of us set off for Frankfurt. After a stay in an air raid shelter a train comes in. So much muddle, party gets split. All railways and transport chaos. Several chances to escape but no food, and feel war will not last much longer. *Very* cold journey to Coblenz; 10 hours for 50 miles; lay in luggage rack.**

**Spend Sunday in Coblenz Castle. Saw Fortress shot down during day. Flat city and no trains. Leave at 6.45 p.m. after repairs to railway, for Frankfurt. Arrive about 11 p.m. Put underground in boiler house with many others. No room; foul smell. Leave at 6 a.m. 26/2/45.**

**Arrive at Oberusel (Sweat Box) at 9 a.m. Put in cells. Searched and interrogated with many threats. Played dumb. Told Tubby (Navigator) and Stan (Rear Gunner) were dead. One of crew told that Eddie (M.U. Gunner) had been killed also.**

One was extremely sad because they were all good friends. One just had to accept it because this was war and there were going to be casualties. I was very sad from the point of view that I had given them time to get out before the aircraft really went out of control. Extremely sad.

**Food, 4 pieces of bread and plate of soup per day. Very hungry. Three days solitary confinement. Severe interrogation by a major; many threats. Honoured by being called a 'fool'. Played quite dumb.**

After I had had a few days solitary confinement in a very cold horrible barracks I went before a German Army officer. I had got engaged just before I started operations. It must have been published in the *Daily Telegraph* or something like that. The first thing he said to me was 'How's Nancy? Is she all right? Is she still in Washington or has she come back to the UK?' Just like that – right out of the blue. He then offered me a cigarette. Eventually he found that he was not going to get any information from me. He told a guard to come in and I was put back in solitary confinement for a couple of days. He had also told me the order we had taken off from Upwood that night.

Three more days solitary. Move out on Saturday evening 3/3/45. 24 hours for 40 miles with no food or water. Railway bombed and engine broke down.

Arrive Dulag Luft on Sunday. Searched. Had first shower and some new clothes. A good feed off Red Cross parcels. Good billets and plenty of company.

6/3/45. Leave Dulag Luft in box cars for Nuremberg. Rations two pieces of bread and a plate of soup per day. Feeling very weak. Sleep on floor with a few wet wood shavings underneath and two blankets. Huts crawling. Three of us sleep together to keep warm. First Red Cross parcel and a 'shower' on 15/3/45. Only rusty tins to eat and drink out of; bowls and cups arrived about two weeks later.

Feel a lot better. Camp getting organised. A few potatoes added to ration.

Next parcel one between four on 18/3/45. Just like children at Christmas. Wish Red Cross personnel could see our joy. Next

**Left** Members of Desmond Pelly's crew, May 1944. From left to right, Thomas Carr (rear gunner), David Sinfield (navigator), Desmond Pelly (pilot), Bill Pearce (radio operator, RAAF), and Reg Morgan (flight engineer).
*(Desmond Pelly)*

Nuremberg. One Red Cross parcel for two men. Travel with Archie (Set Operator) and Joe (Visual Bomb Aimer). Stop 48 hours at Wurzburg. Civilians very hostile. Machine gun turned on us, but guards protected us. Reach Nuremberg after 4 very uncomfortable days with lack of water, cramped conditions (38 to half a box car), 10/3/45.

parcel one each on 20/3/45. A few games and books arrived. The weather a lot better; news good; life a lot more cheerful. Bill (Wireless Operator) in next compound came in 20/3/45.

21/3/45. Life a lot easier with Red Cross parcels. A lot of air activity. Camp filling up from places being evacuated. Some grand weather. Several evacuation scares. Lectures arranged, soft ball games etc. Services by a good Army Padre. Compound very full, mostly Serbs.

3/4/45. Warned that we should leave the camp on foot tomorrow. Plenty of rations prepared and large!! meals cooked so as to start with full stomachs. Complete chaos in camp; many more move into compound.

We realised the war was nearly over. Our troops and the Americans were going right through the continent. We felt that the war was not going to last much longer. Yes we had our doubts, when we were very hungry, but overall we realised we were not going to be prisoners of war very long.

4/4/45. Ready to march by 9 a.m. Set off, well fed, by midday. Bombed and machine gunned by Yank aircraft; 3 killed. Spend first night under a pew in a church. Rather cold. Joe very ill, mostly over my feet! 14 kilometres covered.

5/4/45. On road by 9 a.m. after a fair breakfast. March to Newmarkt. Rest most of afternoon. Line up for two hours in pouring rain and darkness for rations; eventually told there were none left. March on until 3 a.m. Sleep in wood 12 km south of Newmarkt. Very wet and uncomfortable night.

We were told very clearly that if we tried to escape on the march and were caught we would be shot. That was a fair warning so there was no point in escaping because the war was getting closer to the end. The guards were perfectly pleasant to us. They were short of food themselves.

6/4/45. Good breakfast with porridge, on road by 10 a.m. March to Bellingries. Get a Red Cross parcel on the road, and bread. Sleep in church, arrive after dark. Bed of marble slabs covered with very wet blankets. Frozen all night; rather bruised and stiff.

7/4/45. Good meals and good trading with civilians – cigarettes and soap for bread and eggs. Move on at 2 p.m. for 6 km.

Sleep in barn, rather cold, blankets still soaked. Good meals, mostly stolen. Warned on S.S. shooting stragglers.

8/4/45. Aircraft spot us and watch us every two hours. Move off at midday. March 15 km to a pleasant village. Very hot day. Good trading. Sleep in barn, quite good night.

9/4/45. On road by 9 a.m. March 18 km to Neustadt. Red Cross parcel and bread. Plenty of defences around town. Stay a few kms beyond Neustadt in a barn. Plenty of potatoes, quite good trading.

10/4/45. On road by 2 p.m. March 10 km to Sweinbach. Stay two nights. Good wash, plenty to eat. Stomach badly upset, probably on account of eating bad potatoes previous day. Trading with farmers most profitable.

13/4/45. March 9 km to small village. Red Cross parcel between 4. Stomach better. A good night. Move at 2 p.m.

14/4/45. March 10 kms to out-of-way farm; quite comfortable.

15/4/45. Stay here all day. Food running low.

16/4/45. March 4 km. Red Cross parcels. Very little organisation, no one knows where we are going. Another night in barns. Stomach upset by eating out of tins.

17/4/45. Sudden panic; start marching early. 4 km. Still nothing known, so spend another night in barns.

18/4/45. After much waiting around move into Mooseburg. A hot shower and Argentine Red Cross bulk food. Camp very overcrowded. Total German rations on march was half a loaf of bread and half an ounce of honey butter per man.

19/4/45. Camp not too bad. Food fair, growing less each day. Red Cross parcels regular. Crowds coming in from all around. Met several people I know. Life rather boring, but excitement growing as troops get near. B.B.C. news several times a day. Order for P.O.Ws. to remain in one place came just in time before we moved out; only about 2 hours before we were to set out for Innsbruck.

29/4/45. LIBERATED. **Firing heard at breakfast time. Aircraft circling camp all the time. 12 p.m. American flag hoisted over Mooseburg, shortly after over camp. A jeep and tank parade through camp. Mad excitement. Masses of rumours about getting home. Hospital cases flown home.**

2/5/45. **See Robby (A. D. P's late Flight Commander) and have a chat. Tells me we have not been heard of. Sent off 'V' mail and a note by an American.**

3/5/45. **Begin moving out by air. Still a long wait for us.**

4/5/45. **Bad news about evacuation. Obviously no organisation whatever. All feel we have been let down badly, very fed up. Had a bath. Rations improving. Camp in disgusting state, nothing done to keep it clean at all. Food still better.**

7/5/45. **10,000 suddenly move out, everyone feeling more cheerful.**

8/5/45. **Move to Straubing in trucks. End of war. A lot of Germans fly in and give themselves up.**

9/5/45. **Hang around all day. Yank priority on flying out. Very fed up. Very short of water and no sanitary arrangements.**

10/5/45. **Still Yank priority, but fly out late in afternoon to Nancy. A feed and then on to Epinal by train. Grand to see smiling faces again and feel free.**

11/5/45. **Get to bed in early hours of morning. Prisoners' Paradise, everything done for us by Goon (German) prisoners. Plenty to eat, hot shower, de-lousing, new clothes, feel on top of the world. Move out in evening and entrain for Le Havre. Arrive very hungry at American camp 36 hours later. Meal and trucks to Le Havre. Stay there overnight.**

14/5/45. **Fly home to Dunsfold.**

After the war Desmond volunteered to stay in the RAFVR but his hearing was not good and he was demobbed in 1946. 'I was in touch with my navigator's parents. He was an only child – rather devastating for them. I also spoke to the rear gunner's family, from South Africa, who came over to find out what had happened.'

My feeling has always been that I was extremely privileged to be allowed by the Royal Air Force to captain a four-engine aircraft, with a crew of eight, at the age of 21. We had some wonderful times together as a crew. I still keep in touch with my wireless operator in Australia. Morale was good – we did our job professionally. You grew up very quickly. There's no question about that. I have no real regrets. We were doing a job we had to do. RAF Bomber Command and the American Eighth Air Force were the only people who could damage the German war effort at that time. I think, hopefully, that we shortened the war by quite a considerable period. ●

**Left** Retired Bomber Command veteran, Flight Lieutenant Desmond Pelly, DFC. *(Steve Darlow)*

# ACKNOWLEDGEMENTS AND NOTES

**General note**

Readers will notice the reference to both the Pathfinder Force and Path Finder Force in the text. This is because the Pathfinder Force achieved group status in January 1943 and became No. 8 Group Path Finder Force. Within the narrative we have used which ever name applies at that specific stage in time. Readers should also be aware that when quoting direct from veteran sources we have decided to remain true to the source, and retained any quirks of spelling – for example 'Mooseburg' when referring to the town of Moosburg.

**Chapter One** (Sean Feast)

I would like to thank Bill Higgs for his memories of his former skipper, and Johnnie Clifford and the Pathfinder Museum at RAF Wyton for access to Jimmy's personal album.

**Chapter Two** (Julian Evan-Hart)

I would like to thank Tim Hake, Colin Parish, Mr Parish Senior, Steve Parker, who skilfully drove the excavator, Mr and Mrs David Pusey, Squadron Leader A. Swann (EOD), Glynn Morgan, Gareth Jones, Neil Holt (aerial photographs), Simon Parry, Dave King, Melvin Brownless and everyone else involved in assisting with and researching this seemingly long-forgotten wartime incident.

**Chapter Three** (Christopher Yeoman)

After my first visit to Leonard Adlam's grave I began to research the events surrounding his death, and in so doing I came into contact with several sources that proved to be immensely helpful in my pursuit for answers. One such source that ought to be mentioned is Brian J. Rapier and his original research recorded in the out-of-print book *White Rose Base*. Another is Richard Allenby, who for a number of years has studied the airfields, crash sites and aircraft that fell in the Yorkshire countryside. Thanks also to Helen Langfield-Smith for contacting me and, in 2011, for providing the account of the actions of her grandfather, Sergeant Robert Langfield, following the crash of the Whitley on the fateful night.

Irrespective of everything else I have discovered in my search for information relating to Leonard Adlam, the most significant find of all has been his daughter, Delphine. Unexpectedly in April 2010, Delphine Hayes contacted me from Long Island, New York, and introduced herself as Leonard Adlam's daughter. Since our reunion, Delphine has provided me with information and material that I once thought would be improbable to obtain, and for that I am truly privileged to have had the opportunity to learn more about her father.

**Chapter Four** (Sean Feast)
I would like to thank Eddie Blair for details of his father's life, and the work of Mike King in bringing Jack's story to my attention.

**Chapter Five** (Steve Darlow)
John's story is based upon an interview with the author conducted in 2010, and access to some of John's personal papers. I extend my sincerest appreciation to John for sharing his experiences.

**Chapter Six** (Julian Evan-Hart)
Sadly no complete crew photographs of this crew or indeed of Halifax LW682 are known to exist. Some may well have been taken during the war. Indeed, some may well be lying in grandfathers' dusty photo albums somewhere. If anyone knows of any, I would very much like to hear from you.

I would like to thank Cynrik de Decker of the Belgian Aviation History Association, all members of the BAHA involved, Robert Fleming of the No. 426 (Thunderbird) Squadron Association, David King and Kelvin Youngs.

**Chapter Seven** (Steve Darlow)
The accounts of aircrew lost on operations comes from 'K' reports (*Report on Loss of Aircraft on Operations*) held in the AIR 14 files at the National Archives, Kew, London. The quoted Sir Arthur Harris letter is held in the AIR 20 2955 file at the National Archives.

**Chapter Eight** (Adam Purcell)
Much of this chapter was based on wartime letters written by Gilbert Pate to his family. These are in the personal collection of Peggy and Gil Thew, Gilbert's sister and nephew, whom I interviewed in April and August 2010. Also in the archive that Gil and Peggy graciously allowed me to study are photographs and newspaper articles (including one from the *Daily Mail*, 26 April 1944).

Other wartime letters, by Phil Smith to his family and by Sydney Pate to Don Smith, were used courtesy of Phil's widow, Mollie Smith. Also from Mollie was an unpublished manuscript, originally written for Phil's grandson, entitled '*Phil's Recollections of 1939–1945 War*'.

Official records sourced from the National Archives of Australia were Gilbert Pate's RAAF Service Record (NAA: A9301, 423311) and Casualty or Repatriation File (NAA: A705, 166/32/380) and the No. 467 Squadron Operational Record Book (NAA: AWM64, 1/427). Official information from The National Archives (UK) was in Night Raid Report 540 (TNA: PRO AIR 14/3411). I also used the Commonwealth War Graves Commission database; further information was provided by IX (B) Squadron Association historian Roger Audis and No. 49 Squadron historian Colin Cripps.

Books consulted were: Hank Nelson, *Chased by the Sun* (ABC Books, 2002); Leo McKinstry, *Lancaster: The Second World War's Greatest Bomber* (John Murray Publishers (UK), 2009); W. J. Lawrence, *No. 5 Bomber Group RAF (1939–1945)* (Faber and Faber Ltd, London, 1951).

**Chapter Nine** (Steve Darlow)
I would like to express my sincere thanks to Anders Lund, Stuart Matthews and the family of John Ernest Fitzgerald for their help with the article. In addition, thanks are extended to Dr Stephen Davies, Project Director of the Canadian Letters and Images Project.

**Chapter Ten** (Steve Bond)
I would like to thank Jack Bromfield for his tireless patience in recounting in great detail his life-changing experiences in No. 158 Squadron and subsequently as a prisoner of war, plus supporting reminiscences from Hauptmann Heinz Rökker, the nightfighter pilot who shot Jack down. The two of them got on famously when they finally came face to face in 2004.

**Chapter Eleven** (Steve Darlow)
Desmond Pelly was interviewed for this article in 2010, at which point he also made available his personal logbook, photographs and other written reminiscences. I extend my sincerest appreciation to Desmond for sharing his experiences.

# INDEX